MYTHS AND LEGENDS OF

MOUNT OLYMPOS

by
Charles F. Baker III and Rosalie F. Baker

■

illustrated by Joyce Audy Zarins

CONTENTS

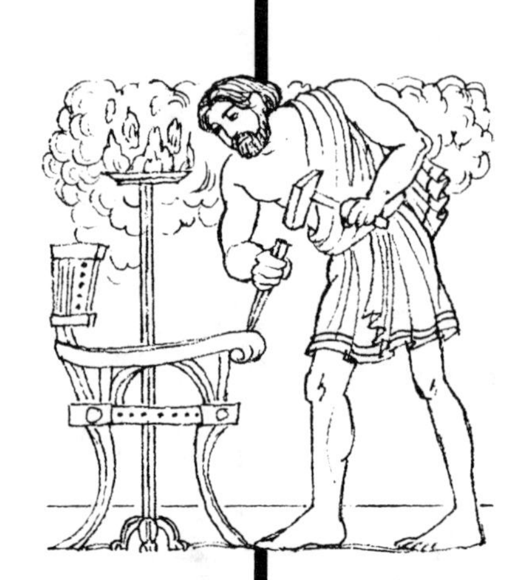

COBBLESTONE Publishing, Inc.
7 School Street
Peterborough, NH 03458

Manufactured in the United States of America
ISBN 0-942389-06-9

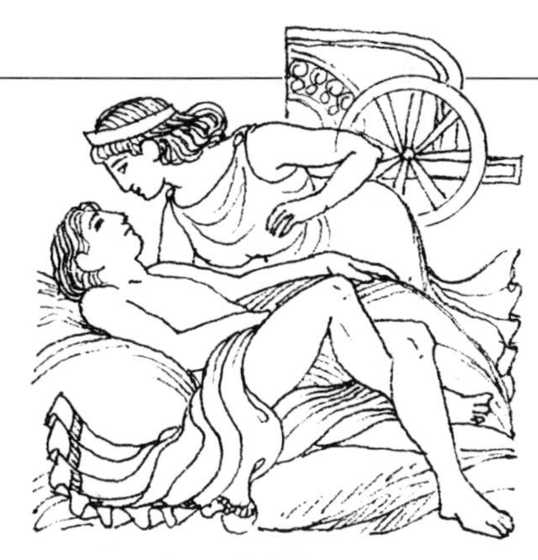

CHAPTER THREE

ADVENTURES OF THE GODS

CHAPTER FOUR

ROMANCE AMONG THE GODS

CHAPTER FIVE

FESTIVALS FOR THE GODS

ABOUT THE COVER

Apollo Pursuing Daphne; Giovanni Battista TIEPOLO; National Gallery of Art, Washington; Samuel H. Kress Collection

Copy-edited by Barbara Jatkola
Designed by C. Porter Designs
Illustrations by Joyce Audy Zarins
Map by Coni Porter
Desktop publishing by Sally Nichols Jacke
Printing and binding by Capital City Press, Inc.

THOSE WHOM THE GODS FAVOR, HUMANS ALSO PRAISE.

Hesiod (fl. c. 700 B.C.), *Theogony*, Fragment 23

The myths of the gods and goddesses of Mount Olympos provide a fascinating glimpse into the beliefs and daily customs of the ancient Greeks and Romans, the forerunners of Western civilization. In the fast-paced world of the twentieth century, when technology and ideas are soon outdated, these tales have proved to be timeless. Even though people no longer follow the religious beliefs they represent, the names of individual deities and the deeds they performed continue to inspire people in all professions. Writers and artists incorporate themes from the myths in their works; scientists name planets, space vehicles, and stars for the deities; psychologists use their actions to analyze and explain certain behavior patterns; and publicity agents promote products using their names as symbols. Sometimes people change the myths to suit their own needs, but these distorted versions are rarely an improvement over the originals.

Part of the reason for these distortions is that the details of many classical myths vary from author to author and area to area. To provide a reasonably comprehensive insight into Greek and Roman mythology, we chose to concentrate on a particular area and subject: the reign of the Olympians, the gods and goddesses of Mount Olympos. Since the ancients spent much time honoring their deities, the last chapter describes a variety of religious festivals celebrated in ancient Greece and Rome. All the stories follow, as closely as possible, the myths as written by the ancients.

The Greeks and Romans often had different names for each deity. We decided to use the Greek names in stories that take place in Greek-speaking areas and are attributed to Greek mythology and the Latin names in stories that take place in Latin-speaking areas and are attributed to Roman mythology. (Since most of these myths were well known in both Greek and Roman societies, the list on page 5 provides the Greek names and their Latin equivalents.) We also chose to follow the Greek spellings in the transliteration of Greek names into English. Hence, we have used *k* rather than *c* in names such as Herakles and Kekrops. We have kept the *os* endings in Greek names (for example, Olympos and Kronos) rather than using the later Latin adaptation *us*. (We have used the *us* endings only in the Roman myths.) The Latin alphabet does not include the letter *j*, so we have used *i* as the Romans did (for example, Iuno and Iupiter). For the names of mythological places, we have transliterated the Greek and Roman names according to the myth. For the names of real places, we have used the English spellings.

Greek Names of the Ancient Gods and Goddesses and Their Roman Equivalents

MYTHOLOGICAL FIGURES

GREEK NAME	ROMAN EQUIVALENT
Aphrodite	Venus
Apollo	Apollo
Ares	Mars
Artemis	Diana
Athena	Minerva
Bakchoi	Bacchants
Bakchos	Bacchus
Demeter	Ceres
Eileithyia	Ilithyia (also Iuno Lucina)
Eos	Aurora
Erinyes	Furies
Eros	Cupid
Gaia (also Ge)	Terra (also Tellus)
Hades (also Pluto)	Dis
Helios	Sol
Hephaestos	Vulcan
Hera	Iuno
Herakles	Hercules
Hermes	Mercury
Hestia	Vesta
Nike	Victory
Persephone	Proserpina
Poseidon	Neptune
Zeus	Iupiter

GREEK NAME	ROMAN EQUIVALENT*
Adrasteia	Adrastea
Alkmene	Alcmena
Alkyoneus	Alcyoneus
Amaltheia	Amalthea
Argos	Argus
Dardanos	Dardanus
Deukalion	Deucalion
Dionysos	Dionysus
Enkelados	Enceladus
Erichthonios	Erichthonius
Hekatoncheires	Hecatoncheires
Inachos	Inachus
Kadmos	Cadmus
Kalliope	Calliope
Kedalion	Cedalion
Kekrops	Cecrops
Keleos	Celeus
Klymene	Clymene
Kyklopes	Cyclopes
Mainades	Maenads
Oinopion	Oenopion
Okeanos	Oceanus
Pandrosos	Pandrosus
Phoibe	Phoebe
Silenos	Silenus
Uranos	Uranus
Zephyros	Zephyrus

**Spelling changes only from Greek to Roman*

ZEUS' PROGENY
BY MORTAL WIVES
ALKMENE
EUROPA
IO
SEMELE
HERAKLES Greek legendary hero
EPAPHOS king of Egypt
DIONYSOS god of wine and the vine
MINOS king of Crete
SARPEDON king of Lycians
OINOPION king of Chios
MEROPE beloved by Orion
RHADAMANTHYS judge in underworld
OUT OF
WHO
NIGHT subduer of gods and mortals
GAIA Earth
NEREUS old god of the sea
TYPHON destructive monster
LADON dragon guardian of golden apples of Hesperides
6 MONSTERS
TITANS
3 HEKATONCHEIRES hundred-handed creatures
3 KYKLOPES one-eyed creatures
TITANS
MNEMOSYNE goddess of memory
OKEANOS god of water
TETHYS
IAPETOS ancestor of the human race
CRIUS
THEMIS goddess of law and justice
MARRY
PALLAS
NIKE goddess of victory
METIS goddess of prudence
INACHOS king of Argos
DORIS water nymph
KLYMENE
MARRY
WITH NEREUS PRODUCES
DEUKALION survivor of the flood
PROMETHEUS
EPIMETHEUS
ATLAS holds world on his shoulders
THETIS water nymph
HESPERIDES guardians of golden apples of Hera
PLEIADES 7 daughters, including Elektra and Maia
ACHILLES Greek hero

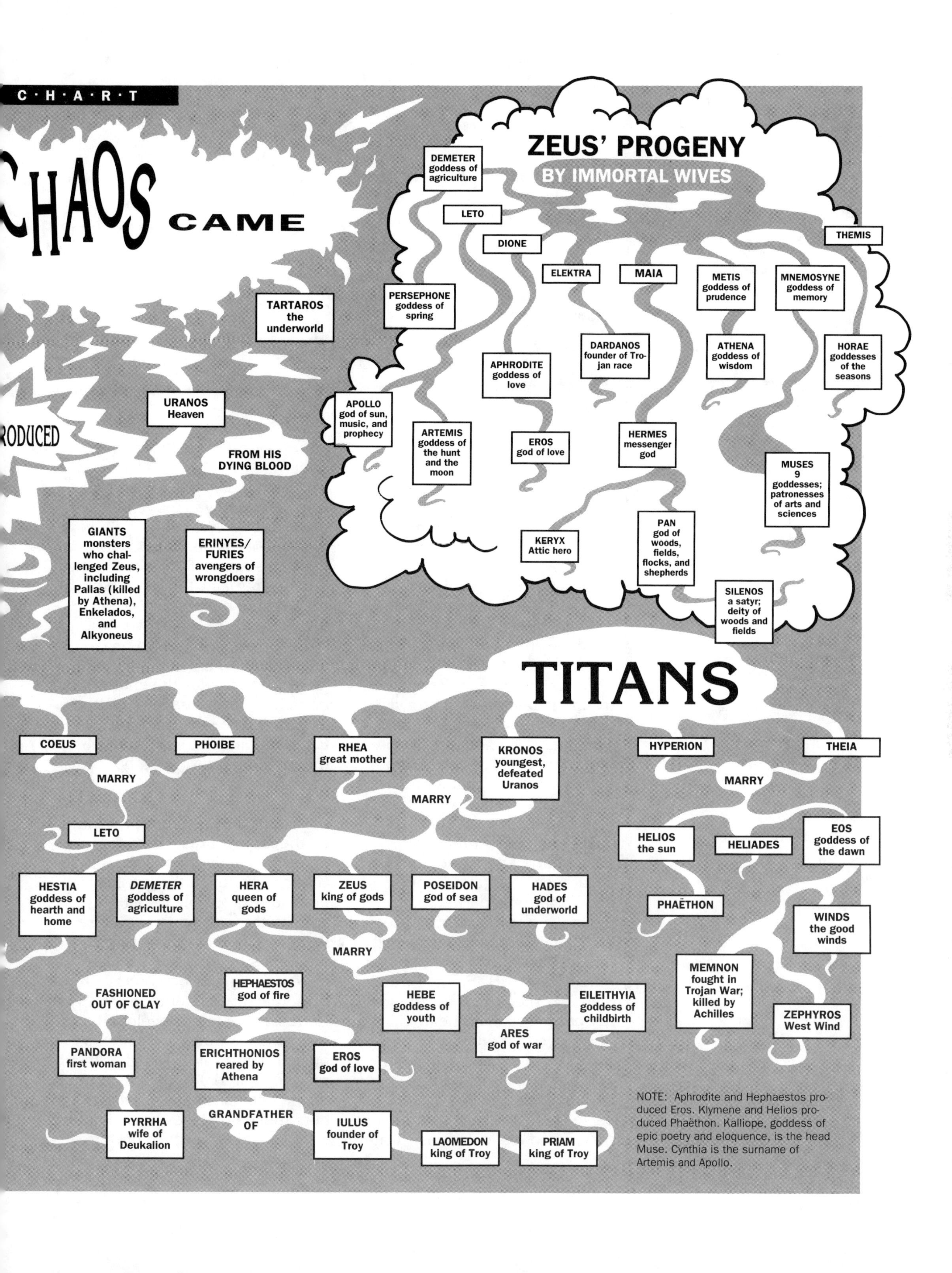
C·H·A·R·T
CHAOS CAME
RODUCED
TARTAROS the underworld
URANOS Heaven
FROM HIS DYING BLOOD
GIANTS monsters who chal-lenged Zeus, including Pallas (killed by Athena), Enkelados, and Alkyoneus
ERINYES/ FURIES avengers of wrongdoers
ZEUS' PROGENY
BY IMMORTAL WIVES
DEMETER goddess of agriculture
LETO
DIONE
ELEKTRA
MAIA
METIS goddess of prudence
MNEMOSYNE goddess of memory
THEMIS
PERSEPHONE goddess of spring
DARDANOS founder of Tro-jan race
ATHENA goddess of wisdom
HORAE goddesses of the seasons
APHRODITE goddess of love
APOLLO god of sun, music, and prophecy
ARTEMIS goddess of the hunt and the moon
EROS god of love
HERMES messenger god
MUSES 9 goddesses; patronesses of arts and sciences
KERYX Attic hero
PAN god of woods, fields, flocks, and shepherds
SILENOS a satyr; deity of woods and fields
TITANS
COEUS
PHOIBE
MARRY
LETO
RHEA great mother
KRONOS youngest, defeated Uranos
MARRY
HYPERION
THEIA
MARRY
HELIOS the sun
HELIADES
EOS goddess of the dawn
HESTIA goddess of hearth and home
DEMETER goddess of agriculture
HERA queen of gods
ZEUS king of gods
POSEIDON god of sea
HADES god of underworld
PHAËTHON
WINDS the good winds
MARRY
FASHIONED OUT OF CLAY
HEPHAESTOS god of fire
HEBE goddess of youth
EILEITHYIA goddess of childbirth
MEMNON fought in Trojan War; killed by Achilles
ZEPHYROS West Wind
ARES god of war
PANDORA first woman
ERICHTHONIOS reared by Athena
EROS god of love
PYRRHA wife of Deukalion
GRANDFATHER OF
IULUS founder of Troy
LAOMEDON king of Troy
PRIAM king of Troy
NOTE: Aphrodite and Hephaestos produced Eros. Klymene and Helios produced Phaëthon. Kalliope, goddess of epic poetry and eloquence, is the head Muse. Cynthia is the surname of Artemis and Apollo.

THE REIGN OF ZEUS

Before Zeus

Today we marvel, and sometimes scoff, at the tales developed by the ancient Greeks to explain the world as they knew it. Yet even with the tremendous amount of information provided by our space explorations and satellite findings, we still debate the answers to these questions: When did the world begin? Who made it? How far does it extend?

According to Greek mythology, in the beginning there was Chaos, a huge mass of matter. The myths did not explain the origin and composition of Chaos, but they did say that it had no form, no divisions, no life. Everywhere was a barren stillness.

To inhabit this great void, Earth came into being, followed by Uranos, the great Heaven, and Tartaros, a dark, gloomy place deep within Earth. (Legend said it would take an anvil thrown from Earth nine days to reach Tartaros.) Still, all was cold and silent until Earth spread her goodness over the land. Then love came into being, as did mountains, seas, day, night, sky, flowers, birds, and trees. Organization entered the universe, as the formless mass separated into distinct areas. Water no longer mixed with land but streamed through it and around it. Heaven distanced itself from Earth. There was movement, life, and beauty. The order and number of events differ according to the ancient source, but the concept remains the same because these shapes accounted for the world as the ancients saw it.

Earth was believed to be circular and flat, a disklike piece of land. Heaven was the enormous domelike cover, made of bronze or iron and reaching down to Earth on all sides. Tartaros was the dark, unknown area beneath the land.

Earth and Heaven were the dominant beings and represented the largest area. Earth's name was Gaia; Heaven's was Uranos. Yet even they could not be held responsible for all the activity throughout the universe. Weather patterns, storms, and the forces of nature all had to have an origin or be controlled by some supernatural power. Hence, more tales developed. Gaia and Uranos were paired as husband and wife. Together they produced an entire generation of divine beings—huge, powerful humanlike creatures known as Titans. Gaia also gave birth to

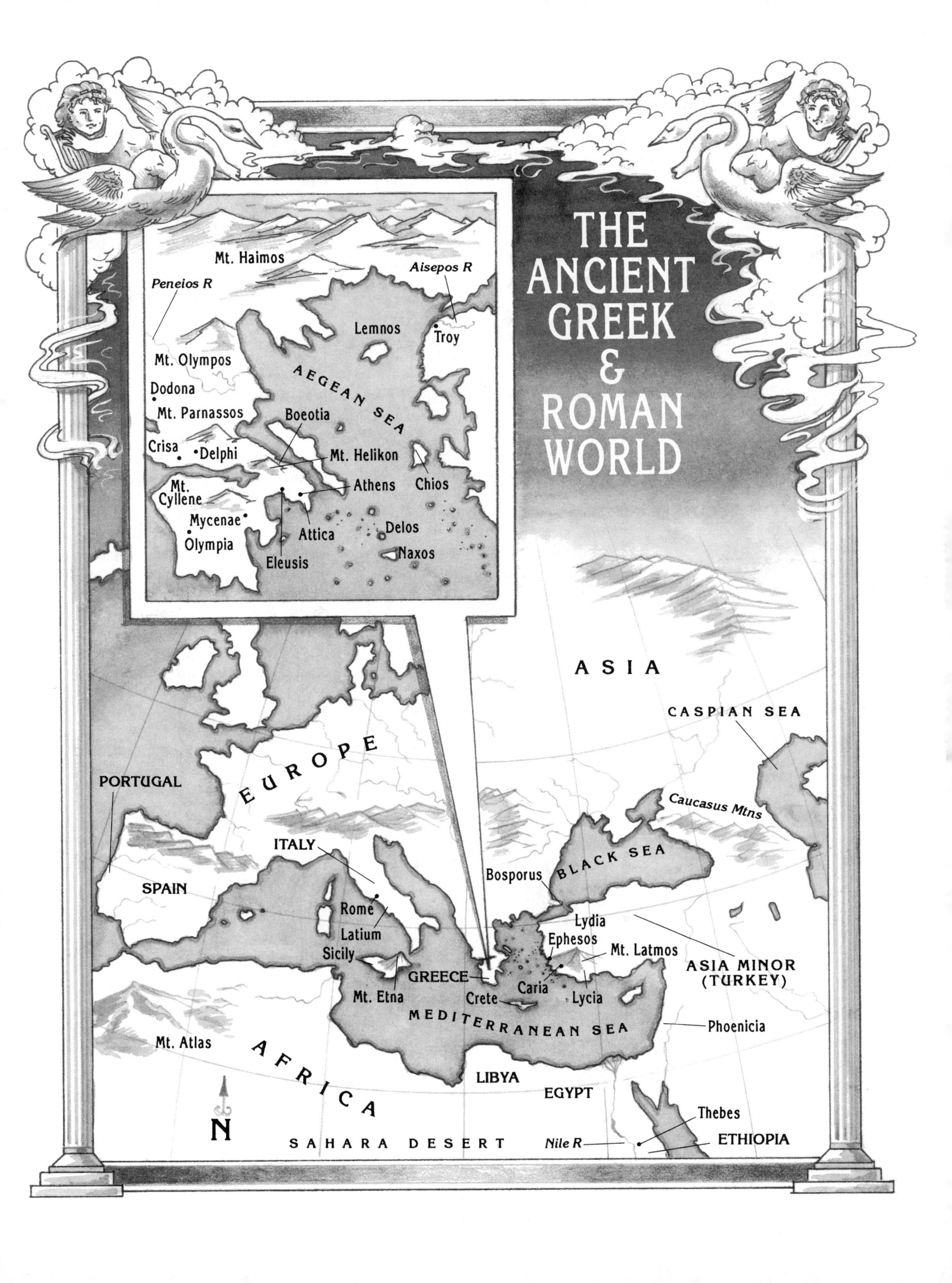
THE ANCIENT GREEK & ROMAN WORLD
Mt. Haimos
Aisepos R
Peneios R
Lemnos
Troy
Mt. Olympos
AEGEAN SEA
Dodona
Mt. Parnassos
Boeotia
Crisa
Delphi
Mt. Helikon
Chios
Athens
Mt. Cyllene
Mycenae
Olympia
Attica
Delos
Naxos
Eleusis
ASIA
CASPIAN SEA
EUROPE
PORTUGAL
Caucasus Mtns
ITALY
BLACK SEA
Bosporus
SPAIN
Rome
Latium
Lydia
Ephesos
Sicily
Mt. Latmos
ASIA MINOR (TURKEY)
GREECE
Caria
Mt. Etna
Crete
Lycia
MEDITERRANEAN SEA
Phoenicia
Mt. Atlas
AFRICA
LIBYA
EGYPT
Thebes
N
SAHARA DESERT
Nile R
ETHIOPIA

URANOS FELL, MORTALLY WOUNDED. BUT BEFORE HE DIED, HE CURSED HIS SON AND PREDICTED THAT KRONOS WOULD FALL.

six horrible monsters—three hundred-handed giants called Hekatoncheires and three one-eyed monsters called Kyklopes.

The forces of the universe were controlled, but all was not harmonious. Uranos was intensely jealous and hated his offspring. According to Greek mythology, he chained them fast within Gaia's enormous mass. (Some sources describe the area as Tartaros.) There they remained, motionless and powerless, until Gaia felt so strained and uncomfortable that she turned within herself and pleaded with her offspring to rise up and defeat the cruel Uranos. Despite their size and strength, the Titans so feared their father that no one dared answer Gaia's tearful pleas—no one except Kronos.

He needed no second urging. Taking a sword in his hand, he waited in hiding until his father came to visit his mother. As Uranos approached, Kronos disentangled himself from the bonds confining him inside Gaia and sprang upon his father. He dealt one quick but fatal blow. Uranos fell, mortally wounded. But before he died, he cursed his son and predicted that Kronos would fall as had his father—at the hands of a son. Kronos paid no heed to his father's curse; he thought only of his siblings and cut the chains confining them. Then, without warning, a horde of huge, fierce men rose from the blood that had gushed forth from Uranos' fatal wound. They were the Giants. They were followed by three winged maidens, whose hair was a mass of writhing serpents and whose eyes dripped blood. These were the Erinyes (also called Eumenides), or Furies.

Kronos surveyed the brood of enormous creatures before him—his brothers and sisters—and took charge, the new ruler of the universe. He confined the Kyklopes and Hekatoncheires to Tartaros. High on Mount Olympos, which the Greeks considered the center of the universe, Kronos made his home. He chose the Titaness Rhea as his queen and assigned to each of his other siblings a section of the universe to govern.

Kronos Dethroned

Kronos enjoyed ruling the universe and was determined that his father's curse (see previous myth) would never come true. Kronos' plan was to destroy each of his children at birth.

When Rhea, his wife, joyfully announced that she was about to give birth to their first child, Kronos went immediately to the birthing room. As soon as the baby was born, Kronos picked up the child and, without warning, swallowed it. Rhea was too shocked at her husband's horrible actions to protest. She knew of the curse, but she never dreamed Kronos would commit such a heinous crime.

Soon thereafter, Rhea became pregnant with her second child. She feared for her unborn child but did not know how to protect it. When Kronos came to assist at the birth, the all-powerful ruler calmly repeated his horrible crime and swallowed his second child. Was Rhea ever to be a mother?

This continued until Rhea became pregnant for the sixth time. She decided that, if she wished to be a mother, she needed a plan. As the time came for her sixth child to be born, Rhea quietly left for Crete, an island in the eastern Mediterranean Sea. But Kronos was not to be deceived. He too went to Crete, confident in his power and prepared to treat the sixth child as he had the first five. Rhea welcomed Kronos warmly and handed him a lovingly swaddled bundle. Kronos quickly took it from Rhea's arms and swallowed it, blanket and all. He asked no questions; he did not even look at his child. He had only one thought—to destroy every threat to his rule. And since he had been successful so many times, he had no reason to doubt Rhea's actions.

But he should have! Rhea had given Kronos no newborn infant but a stone wrapped in swaddling clothes. According to the ancients, Kronos did not notice the difference.

This time it was Rhea's turn to rejoice. Her plan worked, and her child escaped Kronos' stomach. Zeus, the name Rhea gave her child, was safe, hidden in a cave belonging to the nymphs Adrasteia and Io. There he was nourished with milk from the goat Amaltheia. To prevent his cries from reaching Mount Olympos and alerting Kronos that a child still lived, Rhea employed her faithful friends and followers, the Kuretes. These demigods, who lived on Crete, uttered shrieks and howls, chanted war songs, and banged their shields and swords.

Time passed, and Zeus grew into a young adult. In appreciation for the vital nourishment Amaltheia had provided at the most crucial time in his life, Zeus placed her in the sky as a constellation—the Capricorn of the zodiac. Also as a token of his gratitude, Zeus took one of Amaltheia's horns and filled it with fruits and flowers. He then gave it miraculous powers that allowed the horn to be filled continuously with whatever Amaltheia wished. This became today's cornucopia.

Kronos, meanwhile, had begun to suspect he had been deceived. When he learned the truth, he immediately prepared for war. He was determined that his father's curse would never come true, but he underestimated the power, force, and cunning of his only living child. Legend says that on one occasion when Kronos was pursuing Zeus, the latter changed his guardian nymphs into bears and himself into a serpent—the origin of the constellation of the Serpent and the Bears.

When Zeus felt that he was ready to match his strength and wits against his father's, he went to Rhea and asked to be made cupbearer to the great ruler. Rhea approved of her son's plan and spoke to Kronos. The great leader enthusiastically agreed to create the position of cupbearer, completely unaware that his new attendant would be his son. Zeus, unknown and unrecognized by his

THE HEKATONCHEIRES READIED THEIR HUNDRED HANDS TO CAUSE EARTH-QUAKES THROUGH-OUT THE WORLD, WHILE THE GIANT KYKLOPES IMMEDI-ATELY FIRED THEIR FORGES AND READIED THEIR ANVILS TO CREATE WEAPONS FOR ZEUS AND HIS FOLLOWERS.

father, performed his task well and won Kronos' confidence.

Now, Zeus felt, was the time to strike. The next day, when he carefully brought Kronos the cup of nectar (a special liquid drunk only by the gods), the unsuspecting ruler downed the entire contents of the cup. Kronos' aging taste buds did not detect the mustard and salt that had been mixed into the nectar, but hours later, his stomach did.

First came the uncomfortable, burning sensation, then the pain of bloatedness, and then the great heaves. Out popped the stone Kronos had swallowed years earlier, and then came Zeus' five siblings, Hestia, Demeter, Hera, Hades, and Poseidon. What rejoicing there was! The three sisters and two brothers were somewhat pale and smaller than Zeus, but their minds and spirits were alert. Kronos knew he had been deceived a second time and prepared to fight for his life.

The Titans, Kronos' sisters and brothers, and their children fought for Kronos. The five newly sprung deities sided with Zeus. The battle was fierce and raged for ten years with no end in sight. Finally, Zeus sought his grandmother Gaia's advice.

"My grandson, go to Tartaros and free the Kyklopes and the Hekatoncheires. Your father imprisoned them there. Surely they will help you."

Zeus followed her advice and bravely entered the dark, forbidding world of Tartaros. He killed the old jailer and freed the monsters, who eagerly promised to fight the Titans. To restore their strength and revive their appearance, Zeus gave them ambrosia and nectar, the food and drink of the gods.

To show their appreciation, the Hekatoncheires readied their hundred hands to cause earthquakes throughout the world, while the giant Kyklopes immediately fired their forges and readied their anvils to create weapons for Zeus and his followers. For Zeus, as the leader and best strategist, the Kyklopes fashioned thunderbolts; for Hades, they made a helmet that would make him invisible; and for Poseidon, they forged the deadly trident.

The day of the great battle arrived, and the two sides prepared to fight. The Titans were immediately at a disadvantage because Hades, invisible with his helmet, had stolen their arms the previous night. Nevertheless, Atlas, the military leader of the Titans (Kronos was too old), gave the battle cry, and the monstrous creatures attacked. What a clash! The ground quaked and split, the seas whirled and foamed, and the heavens groaned and shook. Zeus took careful aim and hurled the first thunderbolt. The Titans stood still, dazed and unable to move. Zeus did not wait for a reaction. He hurled another and another. Flames shot up everywhere. The rivers began to boil. Yet the Titans did not surrender. Then the Hekatoncheires began to hurl rocks. The barrage from the hundred-handed monsters was too much. Many Titans fell, some from wounds, others from exhaustion.

Zeus and his allies closed ranks. Zeus hurled more thunderbolts while the Hekatoncheires swiftly bound the Titans, including Kronos, with ropes. Zeus decreed that their punishment was everlasting confinement in Tartaros, with the Hekatoncheires as their guards. The Titan Prometheus was spared, for he had counseled Zeus wisely. The Titan Epimetheus also was spared, as he had not fought with the Titans. Atlas, the leader in the battle, was condemned to hold the world on his shoulders for eternity.

The children of Kronos had won. Uranos' prophecy had come true. Lots were cast to determine who would rule what. Zeus won the sky, the mountains, and the earth. Hades took command of the vast area under the world. The dead were his subjects, and the precious gems and metals his treasure. Poseidon received the seas, the rivers, and the streams, as well as the power to rouse the waters and cause great storms on land and sea. Demeter became the goddess of the harvest and all living plants and flowers. Hestia was chosen the goddess of the all-important household fire, which sustained the family and family life. Hera became the protectress of marriage and the home.

Zeus ruled the world of gods and men without fear or cruelty. The new king of gods placed the stone Kronos had swallowed in lieu of the infant Zeus at Delphi in central Greece, the site of Apollo's sacred oracle.* For his wife and queen, Zeus chose Hera, and together they lived high on Mount Olympos in northeastern Greece.

**Historians believe that this stone, which ancient writers claim to have seen at Delphi, was a meteorite.*

The Giants

After Zeus and his allies on Mount Olympos defeated the Titans, the Olympians prepared to rest and regain their strength and spirit. During this time, children were born, and the world above and below was at peace. But this was not to last forever. Gaia, the great mother Earth (Kronos' mother and Zeus' grandmother), had not forgotten the Titans condemned by Zeus to dark Tartaros. She remembered the enormous creatures, known as the Giants, which had sprung from Uranos' blood,* and Gaia persuaded them to avenge their father's cruel dethronement.

Revenge came one day without warning. The Giants attacked Mount Olympos, hurling stones and firebrands with such fury that the Olympians could not regroup to prepare a proper defense.

The Giants feared nothing. They believed they were invincible, since they had eaten the fruit of a certain plant that Gaia had produced especially for them. The powers of this plant were such that the gods were powerless to defeat whoever ate it.

**Some sources attribute the Giants to Gaia.*

Only if a mortal were to help the gods in battle against the Giants would this plant lose its strength. Yet even if a mortal were to help, no Giant would die as long as his body remained within the country of his birth.

Unfortunately for the Giants, Zeus heard about this plant and enlisted the help of his mortal son Herakles. After consulting with Herakles, Zeus forbade the sun, the moon, and the dawn to shine above the plant. Under cover of darkness, Herakles searched until he found the plant, picked it, and carried it to Mount Olympos.

Now the Olympians were ready to begin the battle. The Giants were a fearsome foe with their long hair, shaggy beards, and enormous bodies clothed in the skins of wild beasts. (Later legends pictured them with serpent legs.) As these monstrous creatures advanced, they hurled gigantic rocks and torches made of whole oak trees.

Herakles fought alongside the Olympians. He thought he killed the Giant's leader, Alkyoneus, with his first arrow, but the Giant staggered to his feet. Zeus' daughter, the goddess Athena, shouted, "He lives. This must be his homeland. Quickly, carry him beyond these borders." With great difficulty, the Olympians dragged the enormous creature across the fields to the neighboring province. As soon as they crossed the border, Alkyoneus' body went limp. The first Giant was dead.

But there was no time to rejoice, for the twenty-three other Giants were closing in on the Olympians. Zeus hurled thunderbolt after thunderbolt, slowing but not stopping their advance. Apollo shot one in the eye, and as the Giant bent forward in pain, Apollo called to the mortal Herakles to finish the task with an arrow or a fatal blow of his club. Athena picked up a mountain and hurled it at the Giant Enkelados. Herakles let go an arrow, and Enkelados fell dead, with the mountain above him. The ancients later named this island Sicily.

The Olympians, with Herakles' help, spent the entire day crushing the Giants. One by one they fell, until all twenty-four* lay dead. Zeus and his gods and goddesses had survived the greatest test of their power. The Olympians under the mighty Zeus still reigned on Mount Olympos.

**The number of Giants varies according to the source.*

Typhon

Gaia mourned the death of every Giant, but she refused to concede defeat. With the aid of Tartaros, she produced a creature more fearsome than the Giants—Typhon. His head touched the stars, and his outstretched arms reached across the earth. One hundred snake heads hung from his shoulders, and huge coils of loudly hissing vipers hung from his thighs. His entire body was covered with wings. Fire flashed from his eyes, and flaming rocks burst forth from his mouth. His disheveled hair and straggly beard served to intensify his loathsome appearance.

All the Olympians were terrified, except for Athena, the goddess of wisdom. Athena called her father, Zeus, a coward until he decided to fight Typhon single-handedly. Zeus hurled several thunderbolts, which merely bounced off the monster. Zeus then took his steel sickle and slowly advanced toward Typhon. When he came to within a few feet of Typhon, Zeus rushed forward and lanced him with the sickle. The creature let out a bloodcurdling scream and bent forward. "I have wounded him," Zeus shouted. "Let me strike again, for surely I can destroy him."

But such was not the case. Typhon was still too strong for Zeus. The Giant took the coils from around his waist and wound them around Zeus until the Olympian could not move. Then, using Zeus' own sickle, Typhon cut and removed the tendons from the god's legs. He hid them in a cave and ordered the dragon Delphyne, who was half girl and half wild animal, to guard the entrance. He hid Zeus in another cave.

Zeus was helpless. Fortunately, his son Hermes, the messenger of the gods, had witnessed the fight and with help from his fellow gods tricked the dragon and stole the tendons. Hermes carefully replaced them in his father's maimed and bruised limbs.

Zeus's recovery was almost instantaneous. He quickly returned to Mount Olympos to fetch his thunderbolts, and then the chase began.

When Typhon reached Mount Nysa, in northeastern Greece, he was ravenously hungry. The inhabitants, who were friends of the Olympians, tricked the enor-

ZEUS' NAME MEANT "THE ALL POWERFUL," "THE LIGHT," "THE HEAVENS." HE LIVED IN A SPLENDID PLACE HIGH ON MOUNT OLYMPOS, FROM WHICH HE COULD OVERSEE AND RULE THE LIVES AND DEEDS OF BOTH GODS AND HUMANS.

mous creature into eating food that was for mortals alone. Within minutes, Typhon's strength began to ebb. Yet the monster still fought furiously and viciously. He shed so much blood that the ancient Greeks named the mountain on which they battled Mount Haimos. (Haima is the Greek word for "blood.")

When Typhon realized defeat was imminent, he summoned all the strength left in his sagging body and fled to Sicily. Zeus followed. Taking Mount Etna in his hand, he hurled it onto Typhon. The monster was imprisoned at last, and Zeus reigned supreme. According to the ancients, Typhon did not die. Whenever he shifts the weight of the heavy mountain on top of him or whenever he feels angry, his movements cause the insides of Mount Etna to boil over the top and destroy the surrounding countryside.

Great Zeus

The ancient Greeks assigned to Zeus all the characteristics and attributes worthy of so mighty and powerful a deity. His name meant "the all powerful," "the light," "the heavens." He lived in a splendid place high on Mount Olympos, from which he could oversee and rule the lives and deeds of both gods and humans. Law and order were subject to him.

At Dodona, in northwestern Greece, priestesses cared for his temple and oracle, the oldest and most sacred in Greece. Worshipers came to ask the great god's advice and listened to the wind rustling through the oak trees for their answers. Zeus' queen was Hera, but the ancients also associated him with other goddesses and mortal women. He fathered many children, some immortal and others mortal but renowned for their heroic deeds.

Zeus also was worshiped as the all-powerful weather god. Across his chest he wore a fearsome breastplate—a menacing storm cloud, called the aegis, which Hephaestos, the god of fire, had fashioned for him. Zeus had only to shake the aegis to create a wild storm. The ancient artists usually represented it as the skin of a gray goat. His chariot created thunder, and in his hand he held deadly thunderbolts. The powerful eagle was his special messenger, and the hardiest of trees, the oak, was sacred to him.

The famed sculptor Phidias crafted a statue that became one of the seven wonders of the ancient world. At Olympia, in southwestern Greece, the statue sat in an enormous temple. Over a framework of wood, Phidias used ivory to represent the great god's flesh and gold for his garments. In one hand, Zeus held a scepter, a symbol of power, and in the other a statue of the goddess Nike (Victory).

The Gifts of Prometheus and Epimetheus

PROMETHEUS

According to Greek and Roman mythology, after the Olympians defeated the Titans, they assumed control of the land, the air, and the sea. As punishment for their bold attempt to defeat the Olympians, the Titans were condemned forever to Tartaros in the underworld.

In this great struggle, however, one Titan, Prometheus, had sided with Zeus. Why did he commit such a seemingly traitorous deed? At birth, Prometheus was given the power to know the future, and he foresaw the eventual destruction of the Titans. In appreciation for the aid of Prometheus and his brother Epimetheus, Zeus allowed them to remain on earth. Furthermore, he assigned them two extremely important tasks: (1) the creation of animals and humans and (2) equipping these beings with the characteristics essential to survival.

Epimetheus, whose name means "afterthought," immediately undertook the creation of animals. But, as his name implies, he acted without any plans.

Meanwhile, Prometheus, whose name means "forethought," carefully developed his creation and was ready to begin molding the first man. Unfortunately, when Prometheus went to seek the characteristics and skills he required, he discovered that Epimetheus had taken them all. Wings had been given to birds, protective shells to crabs, and legs made for swiftness to deer. Nothing was left! What was Prometheus to do?

Legend tells us that as this great Titan took clay (or earth) and water in his hand and molded the first man, he resolved that instead of making him walk on four legs, as did the animals, his creation would walk like the gods, on two legs.

Prometheus also was determined to give humans another gift that would enable them to improve and develop the world in which they lived. Stealthily, he crept into the chambers of the Olympian god of fire, Hephaestos, and stole a few precious flames from the hearth to give to his new creation. Now all was possible; civilization could advance!

The Olympians, especially Zeus, begrudged humans this special gift. The gods were not ready for mankind to progress too rapidly. Therefore, Zeus ordered that all mortals should sacrifice to the gods on a regular basis. But what should they sacrifice?

Prometheus was ordered to present possible solutions to this dilemma at a meeting of all the Olympians. On the appointed day, Prometheus sacrificed an ox. He then placed two vessels before the great Zeus. One contained the delicious meat of the ox covered by the thick, rough hide; the other held the bare bones covered with the juicy, moist fat. At first Zeus, the judge

ZEUS ORDERED THAT PROMETHEUS BE CHAINED TO THE RUGGED CAUCASUS MOUNTAINS BETWEEN THE BLACK AND CASPIAN SEAS.

of which portion the gods would accept, pointed to the fat-covered container. Then he paused, for he recognized Prometheus' deceitful trick. After a moment's hesitation, he again chose the fat-covered container.

Zeus resolved to make all mortals regret Prometheus' attempt to deceive the great king of the gods. "I shall deprive them of their fire," he thought. "Although they have the meat of their sacrifices and we have only the bones, they will not be able to cook the meat."

Prometheus had witnessed all these events and again resolved to steal fire. He crept into Hephaestos' chamber once more. Placing a flame in the hollow stem of a reed and blocking both ends of the reed with clay so that the flame would smoulder and not die, he quietly left Mount Olympos. Again he presented his mortal friends with fire, and civilization continued to advance.

Soon thereafter, Prometheus was summoned before Zeus. The bargain they had struck at the first meeting remained the same. Mortals were to sacrifice the bones and entrails of animals—a practice that the ancient Greeks and Romans continued to observe for centuries. In addition, Zeus promised never again to deprive mankind of fire. But Prometheus was to be severely punished for giving humans fire.

Zeus ordered that Prometheus be chained to the rugged Caucasus Mountains between the Black and Caspian seas. There one of Zeus' birds, a gigantic eagle, would devour Prometheus' liver every day. At night, his liver would miraculously restore itself, only to be eaten again the following day.

Some ancient writers said that for Prometheus to obtain his freedom, he had only to disclose to Zeus a certain secret that would greatly affect Zeus' life. This secret was that whichever god married the goddess Thetis would be dethroned by the son she would bear him. Despite the horrible pain of his perpetual torture, Prometheus refused Zeus' pleas to disclose this information.

Finally, Prometheus relented, and Zeus allowed his son Herakles to prove his great skill by killing the wretched eagle. The great benefactor of mankind was finally free.

EPIMETHEUS

Angered because he had promised Prometheus that he would not deprive mankind of fire a second time and unwilling to break his oath, Zeus considered other punishments he could inflict on the human race. Then he remembered Epimetheus, who, unlike his brother, reacted first and thought later.

Zeus walked to Hephaestos' chamber and ordered the god of fire to fashion a woman out of clay. Zeus then had each Olympian endow this beautiful mortal with a special gift. One gave her grace, another wit, another boldness, another intelligence, and another beauty. They named her Pandora, which means "all gifted." Zeus entrusted this godlike maiden to his son, the messenger god Hermes, with instructions that he present Pandora as a gift to Epimetheus.

Before Pandora left Mount Olympos, the gods presented her with a sealed box as a marriage gift to her husband. Once settled in Epimetheus' home, Pandora began to wonder about the con-

PANDORA RAN TO THE BOX AND SLOWLY LIFTED THE LID. THE CONTENTS, WHICH HAD BEEN IMPRISONED FOR SO LONG, FORCED ASIDE THE COVER OF THE BOX.

tents of the box. Perhaps some object of great value lay hidden inside. Finally, Pandora's curiosity overwhelmed her.

She ran to the box and slowly lifted the lid. The contents, which had been imprisoned for so long, forced aside the cover of the box. Out flew disease, work, pain, and all the troubles and tragedies that have since that day befallen mankind.

Pandora stood in wonder as the tiny winged evils escaped from their prison. As soon as she realized what was happening, she placed the top on the box—but not before every misfortune had escaped. As Pandora covered the box, she realized that she had managed to keep only one little winged creature inside—hope. Thus, through the centuries, humans have always had the ability to overcome whatever difficulties befall them because they possess hope.

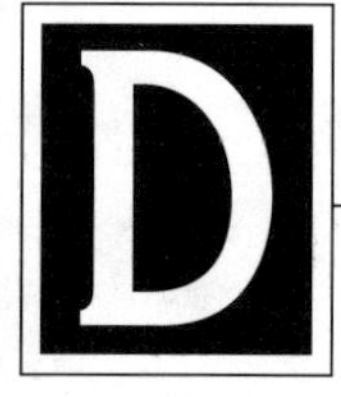

Deukalion and Pyrrha

How and when was the human race created? These questions continually plagued the ancient Greeks. Their attempts to solve these mysteries resulted in the development of several mythological tales, including that of Deukalion and Pyrrha. The Romans later adopted this Greek tale, adding a few details of their own.

The ancients believed that several ages of mankind had existed after the creation of the world. The first was the Golden Age, in which no feuds ever arose, the earth of itself produced food and flowers, and rivers flowed with milk and wine. Next came the Silver Age, in which the seasons of the year began, houses were needed, and mortals had to farm the land. Third was the Bronze Age, in which feuds became commonplace and anger ruled the hearts of many. Finally, during the Iron Age, crime and fraud spread across the earth. So terrible was this fourth period that Zeus decided to intervene.

According to some sources, each age represented an attempt by Zeus to create the best type of human being to inhabit the earth. Others maintain that Zeus created only the first three races and that the formation of the fourth was the work of Prometheus. The supporters of the second theory argue that the humans of the Iron Age had flaws in their make-up because someone other than Zeus had created them. Indeed, the constant strife and recklessness of the people of the Iron Age so angered Zeus that he sought some means by which to destroy them and create a new race that would be worthier of the gift of life.

Zeus summoned all the gods to attend a great council meeting on Mount Olympos. There was much discussion as to the manner of destruction. Zeus knew that if he were to destroy the earth by using his usual manner of punishment, he would need so many bolts of thunder and lightning that the resulting fire might even scorch the heavens. Finally, a decision was made that the earth should be covered with tremendous amounts of water.

Zeus first imprisoned the gentle North Wind and let loose the storm-bearing South Wind to roam unbridled throughout the world. The latter flew with drenched wings, his dreadful shape clothed in darkness, his beard heavy with rain, his hair pouring forth water, his brow supporting the clouds, and his clothes dripping with moisture. As he pressed the hanging clouds with his broad hands, torrents of rain poured forth.

Still not content, and aware that more water was needed to drown the earth, Zeus appealed for help to his brother Poseidon, the god of the sea. Without hesitating, Poseidon struck the earth with his trident. The land trembled and then opened to allow water to burst forth from the depths of the earth.

Soon all became sea, except for an occasional mountain peak rising above the flood. Many people tried to escape to these peaks by fashioning rafts and boats, but the wind and the waves prevented them from reaching any refuge.

Fish, trying to swim with the current, became entangled in the submerged branches of the elm trees. Dolphins shook the oak trees as they swam against them. Aloft in the skies, birds searched for a spot to land, until their weary wings could no longer support them and they fell into the sea. A wolf was seen among a flock of sheep, all striving together for safety, which was nowhere to be found.

For nine days and nine nights, torrential rains pelted the earth, until all life appeared to have ceased. When the Olympians looked down to survey the results of the storm, they spied a small boat shaped like an ark. On board were two individuals.

Without warning, the ark ran aground on Mount Parnassos, in central Greece. Once they realized that Delphi, one of the most sacred areas in the Greek world, lay submerged beneath them, the lone survivors offered prayers to Themis, the patroness of Delphi in early times and the goddess of justice.

As Zeus watched the pious couple at prayer, he recognized them as Deukalion and Pyrrha, the two most devout and just individuals who had inhabited the world. Deukalion's father, Prometheus, had known of the flood and had advised his son to build an ark for himself and his wife, Pyrrha, the daughter of Pandora, considered by many to have been the first woman.

The mighty Olympian's anger gradually subsided as he observed the distressed couple. Quickly, he unlocked the gates confining the gentle North Wind. Within minutes, the storm clouds were dispelled. Zeus then summoned the sea god Triton, who immediately rose from the deep, his shoulders encrusted with shells. Zeus ordered him to blow into his conch shell, the signal for the waters and rivers to recede. As the resounding call to retreat echoed throughout

"LEAVE MY TEMPLE, O MOST PIOUS COUPLE; COVER YOUR HEADS, LOOSEN YOUR GARMENTS, AND THEN TOSS THE BONES OF YOUR MOTHER BEHIND YOU."

the earth, the land gradually emerged from her watery bed. Rivers once again ran in their channels, and the waves of the sea washed only the shoreline.

Yet Deukalion and Pyrrha did not rejoice, for the earth was now deprived of life. All was covered with mud and slime. The silence was deafening. Doubtful as to whether anything might survive, they let loose, as they had on previous days, a dove. When the bird did not return, the weary couple rejoiced, for they knew that their dove had found a home and food.

Again, Deukalion and Pyrrha decided to offer prayers and sacrifices to Themis. Through the slime-covered and stained portals of her temple, they entered into the sacred sanctuary, where the eternal fires no longer burned. "If the anger of the gods may be softened by just prayers, let us know how we might remedy the loss of the human race," they prayed.

Themis heard their pleas and was moved. "Leave my temple, O most pious couple; cover your heads, loosen your garments, and then toss the bones of your mother behind you." Deukalion and Pyrrha waited for the goddess to continue but did not hear another word. What did the words mean? Surely following such a command concerning the revered remains of their mother would be an act of disrespect. Slowly, the couple walked from the temple across the deserted fields. They spent much time discussing the oracle. Finally, Deukalion thought he understood Themis' words.

"Pyrrha," he said, "the earth is the mother of us all, and her bones must be the stones. Therefore, let us cast stones behind our backs." Pyrrha was not at all sure that the oracle had meant this, but certainly something had to be done. Following Themis' commands, the two covered their heads (an ancient custom observed by those making sacrifices) and loosened their garments. Carefully and with a fear of the unknown, Deukalion picked up a stone and cast it over his shoulder. Pyrrha did likewise. Deukalion found another stone and cast it behind him. Pyrrha followed her husband. Again and again, the couple repeated their actions.

When they turned to see what, if anything, was happening, they marveled at the sight. Each stone was turning into a human being—those cast by Deukalion into men, those by Pyrrha into women. The devout couple stood transfixed, hardly able to believe their eyes. The part of the stone that was damp from resting on the earth became flesh, while the rest changed into bone. The veins of the stone remained veins in the newly assumed body.

As the sun rewarmed the earth, the soggy marshes and wetlands began to swell and, of their own accord, nourished the seeds of all that mankind needed to survive. In time, the fields poured forth vegetables, the trees fruit, and the plants flowers.

Zeus, content with all that had happened, vowed not to wreak such havoc and destruction again. The mighty Olympian never had to retract his promise, for this new race of human beings, our ancestors, was kinder, more tolerant, and more worthy of the gift of life.

BEFORE ZEUS

1. Who was Earth? Who was Heaven? How did the ancients picture their world?
2. Who or what produced the Giants?
3. What did Tartaros—the dark, unknown area beneath Earth—become for the ancients and why?
4. Why was Earth, the divine being, credited with making the cold land productive?
5. Why do you think the ancients believed that the offspring of Earth and Heaven were monstrous creatures?

KRONOS DETHRONED

1. How did Rhea save Zeus from Kronos?
2. How did the Kyklopes thank Zeus for freeing them?
3. Why was Atlas' punishment appropriate?
4. After Zeus became cupbearer to Kronos, why did he not poison and kill his father?
5. Should Zeus' brother Hades have been content to rule Tartaros, the area awarded to him?

THE GIANTS/ TYPHON

1. What was the Giants' chief weapon against the Olympians?
2. Who convinced Zeus to challenge Typhon and how?
3. Why was Gaia's plant defense for the Titans appropriate?
4. Was removing Zeus' leg tendons Typhon's best option?
5. What do you think is significant about the fact that no Giant would die as long as his body remained in the country of his birth?

THE GIFTS OF PROMETHEUS AND EPIMETHEUS

1. What was Prometheus' special gift to humans? Why did he give this gift?
2. Whom did the ancients credit with creating the first woman? How did they believe it was done?
3. When Prometheus disguised the ox's bones with juicy fat, was he being deceitful? Why?
4. Why was Zeus determined to make the mortals created by Prometheus sacrifice to the Olympians?
5. Why did the ancients believe that hope was in Pandora's box, and why did it alone not escape?

DEUKALION AND PYRRHA

1. Why did Zeus use water and not fire to destroy the earth?
2. How had Deukalion known to construct a sturdy vessel to withstand the great flood?
3. Why was Zeus so determined to destroy the people who lived during the Iron Age?
4. Why did Deukalion and Pyrrha (and later the ancients themselves) cover their heads as they sacrificed to the gods?
5. Why did the ancients think that Deukalion's ark settled on Mount Parnassos at Delphi?

QUESTIONS FOR DISCUSSION

1. How do the myths of the ancients reflect their belief that Gaia, the great mother Earth, was the life force?
2. Trace Prometheus' role with regard to the development of the human race.

SUGGESTED ACTIVITY

Create a diorama, poster, or model of the world as conceived by the ancients. Include the monstrous inhabitants of each region, Mount Olympos, and Prometheus chained to the rocks. Check the map on page 9 for the location of these sites.

CHILDREN OF THE OLYMPIANS

Mars

The Romans called the god of war Mars. The Greeks referred to him as Ares, but, as they were not a warlike people, his worship was not widespread. The Romans considered Mars their patron god. Soldiers believed that Mars, under the name Gradivus, marched in person at the head of the army, leading them to victory.

The Greek poet Homer says that once when Ares fell to the ground, his body covered almost two acres. It is also said that when a Greek warrior named Diomedes wounded Ares in battle, his cry of pain sounded like the roar of ten thousand charging warriors.

Mars was the son of Iupiter,

the king of the gods, and Iuno, the queen of the gods. He loved the battlefield. In a magnificent suit of shining armor and a helmet adorned with a plume, he rode in a chariot led by four spirited horses. On his arm was an intricately carved shield, and he held a spear ready to be thrown. The Romans thought him invincible, but he was not.

On one occasion, the Aloadae, twin giants, forced him to surrender. These two boys, only nine years old and quite mischievous, decided to prove their strength. They thought, "Why not capture the great god of war?" Their size alone would help them. Each boy was about eighty-one feet tall. They grew at a rate of nine inches every month. How could Mars resist this challenge?

The Aloadae tied Mars with iron chains slipped through iron rings. They kept him prisoner for fifteen months, until the god Mercury freed him. Mars promptly ordered that the giants be killed for their reckless deed.

Hephaestos: The God of Fire

"How could I, Hera, the queen of gods and men, have produced such a weakling? What went wrong? My husband, Zeus, created the majestic and powerful Athena, the goddess of wisdom, without my aid. I only wanted to equal his feat and produce a worthy offspring without his aid. And I did! But look at him with his lame leg! I shall be the laughingstock of Mount Olympos. I cannot let that happen. Hephaestos, my young one, down to earth you must go, and there you must stay. You are not fit to live with us on Mount Olympos."

Poor little Hephaestos! He had barely adjusted his eyes to his bright new royal surroundings when he felt himself tumbling through the air. Splash! Into the water he fell. Fortunately for Hephaestos, the sea nymphs Thetis and Eurynome had watched the terrible incident and eased his fall. Gratefully, he accepted their invitation to live with them and remained there for nine years.

Hephaestos was happy living near the water's edge. Only when he tried to move quickly or to maneuver himself into some narrow spot did he remember that awful day so many years ago when his mother, Hera, had treated him so cruelly. His lame leg would never let him forget.*

One day Hephaestos devised an evil plan. He spent every day, as usual, in his workshop, but now he went much earlier and left later. Thetis and Eurynome began to worry about him. They

**Some sources maintain that Hephaestos was born lame; others say that Hera tossed him out because he was ugly and a weakling and that his lameness was caused by his fall.*

HEPHAESTOS REJOICED WHEN HE HEARD THAT THE CHAINS HE HAD CAREFULLY ATTACHED TO THE CHAIR HAD ENCIRCLED HIS MOTHER'S BODY AS THEY HAD BEEN COMMANDED.

greatly appreciated all the beautiful works of art and ornaments he made for them, but they felt uneasy. Something in his manner had changed.

After several months of this intense work schedule, Hephaestos invited the two sea nymphs to see his newest creation—a beautifully wrought golden chair. "A present for my mother," Hephaestos announced.

Again a sense of uneasiness came over Thetis and Eurynome. "He detests his mother. Why, after all these years, did he spend so much time making such a beautiful gift for her?" they wondered.

Although Hera regretted her rash act, she had never tried to visit Hephaestos or even speak to him. "Why is he sending me such a beautiful present?" she asked herself. "Should I accept it?"

As she gently sat on the thronelike chair, she realized that she had been tricked. On all sides she felt invisible chains twisting around her limbs. Within seconds, she could not move.

Hephaestos' plan of revenge had worked. He rejoiced when he heard that the chains he had carefully attached to the chair had encircled his mother's body as they had been commanded. He laughed when he learned how many unsuccessful attempts were being made to free the queen of the gods. Only he knew the secret of the chains.

Ares, the great Greek god of war, was sent to summon Hephaestos to Mount Olympos. But the lame god had no intention of obeying. Why should he? When he saw Ares approaching, he went to meet him, holding a blazing torch in his hand. The god of war saw the flames, felt its tremendous heat, and quickly returned to Olympos, his mission unaccomplished. Meanwhile, the angry Hera sat motionless in her golden prison.

Next, the jovial and carefree god of wine, Dionysos, was summoned to Olympos and given the task of fetching Hephaestos. Dionysos merrily approached Hephaestos' abode. He paid no attention to Hephaestos' torch and invited Hephaestos to drink with him.

Hephaestos knew why Dionysos

HIGHLIGHT

The Queen of Mount Olympos

The Greeks knew her as Hera. The Romans called her Iuno. She was the wife of the king of the gods, the Greek Zeus and the Roman Iupiter. One legend tells us that to woo her, Zeus disguised himself as a cuckoo, for he felt that she could not resist loving such a cute bird. Then, assuming his godly form, he asked her to become the queen of the gods. This marriage was celebrated with great festivities on Mount Olympos. Soon thereafter, the gods decreed that Hera become the patroness of marriage.

Marriage to Zeus was quite frustrating, since he was not always faithful to his wife. Because she was jealous of her husband's female friends, Hera frequently punished them and their children. Consequently, many writers have portrayed Hera as a wrathful goddess.

To watch her husband's activities and to protect and aid the women who constantly asked for her advice, Hera needed a messenger to help relay her thoughts to the mortals on earth. She chose the goddess Iris. So quickly did Iris travel between earth and Mount Olympos that were it not for her many-colored robe that trailed behind her in the sky, creating a rainbow effect, no one would have known that Iris had passed.

had come, but Dionysos' manner was so friendly that Hephaestos could not refuse him. Hephaestos had never drunk much wine and was unaccustomed to its effects. He drank whatever Dionysos poured and soon happily accompanied his drinking mate to Mount Olympos. There Dionysos persuaded him to loosen his mother's bonds.

Mother and son once again faced each other. Hera apologized for behaving so cruelly toward him, and Hephaestos forgave his mother. All went well until Hera quarreled with her husband, Zeus. Hephaestos so angered Zeus because he sided with his mother that Zeus took him by the foot and threw him from Olympos.

"All day I flew, and at sunset I fell on Lemnos," Hephaestos said. There the inhabitants of the island, the Sentians, nursed his wounds.

Although Zeus had not forbidden Hephaestos to return, the lame god did not seem eager to spend much time on Mount Olympos. Lemnos became his home. He also enjoyed the peaceful, secluded workshops he had fashioned in various parts of the world.

Yet Hephaestos could not forget the gods, for they were always seeking his assistance and skill. No one worked the forge, anvil, and hammer as well as he. The splendid palaces of the gods attested to his skill, as did Zeus' shield, Athena's weapons, and the armor of the Greek hero Achilles. From Hephaestos' forge, Prometheus stole the fire to give to mankind. On Zeus' order to fashion something to plague man, Hephaestos made Pandora, the first woman.

Hephaestos was the blacksmith of the gods and was worshiped as the god of fire. Whenever a volcano spewed forth lava, flames, or smoke, people would say, "The god of fire is working at his forge." When the hearth fire crackled, they said, "Hephaestos is laughing." The island of Lemnos was the center of his volcanic activity. The rumblings and tremors of the earth, especially around Vesuvius in Italy and Etna in Sicily, were thought to be caused by his hammer and bellows and those of his fellow workers in the workshops below.

In art, the ancients usually depicted the god of fire at his forge, with a tunic covering his left shoulder, a great beard, and an enormous frame. But the Greek poet Homer's vivid description of Thetis' visit to Hephaestos' home paints the clearest picture of the ancient god:*

"Thetis of the silver feet came to the house of Hephaestos imperishable, starlike, and shining among the immortals, built of bronze for himself by himself, the god of the dragging footsteps. She found him sweating and toiling busily at his bellows, for he was forging twenty tripods, which were to stand around the wall of his strong-founded hall. Beneath the base of each he had set golden wheels so that of their own motion they could wheel into the assembly of the gods and return again to his house. These were finished, except for the elaborate handles, which

Thetis approached Hephaestos to fashion arms for her son Achilles so that he could fight in the Trojan War. Achilles' friend Patroklos had worn Achilles' armor into battle and been killed. The Trojans had confiscated the dead Greek's arms, leaving Achilles without armor or weapons. This description is from the Iliad.

"WHAT NOW?" THOUGHT HERMES. "NO CRADLE FOR ME—THAT'S FOR SURE!" JUST THEN, HE SAW A HERD OF CATTLE IN THE DISTANCE. "FOOD," HE THOUGHT, "AND AM I HUNGRY." WITHOUT DELAY, HERMES HEADED TOWARD THE CATTLE.

were not yet ready. He was forging these and welding chains. . . . He rose from the anvil, limping, a huge body, but his shrunken legs moved nimbly. He set the bellows away from the fire; all his tools he gathered and put away in a silver chest. With a sponge he wiped his face, hands, sturdy neck, and hairy chest, put on his tunic, took a heavy stick in his hand, and went limping to the doorway. Supporting their master were handmaidens of gold, who looked like living young women. They had intelligence and strength and were able to speak. From the immortal gods they had learned how to do all things."

The Inventive Hermes

According to the ancients, the god Hermes became an inventor at quite an early age. Hermes was born at dawn in a cave far removed from gods and humans. His mother was the nymph Maia, and his father, Zeus, was the king of the gods.

When only hours old, Hermes grew restless and stealthily crept from his cradle and out of his cave in search of adventure. When he spied a turtle slowly making its way across a nearby field, he crept as quickly as he could, lifted the startled creature, and carefully scooped out the turtle's body before sending the homeless animal on its way.

After studying the empty shell for a few minutes, Hermes set to work. He crawled back across the field to fetch an ox hide he had noticed lying on the ground and pulled the skin tightly across the back of the shell. He attached two animal horns to the top of the shell, then stretched seven strings across the shell and the horns. As he plucked each string with his fingers, he was amazed at the beautiful sounds they produced. Hermes called his new toy the lyre.

"What now?" thought the little god. "No cradle for me—that's for sure!" Just then, he saw a herd of cattle in the distance. "Food," he thought, "and am I hungry." Without delay, Hermes headed toward the cattle. His strategy was simple. By shouting and calling, he separated fifty head from the herd and tied boughs of leafy branches to each of their hoofs. To make absolutely sure that no one would follow his tracks, he wove sandals for his own feet, then drove the fifty cattle backward across the field to the banks of a nearby river. After driving the cattle across to the opposite shore, he roasted and ate two of them.

"I must return before I'm found to be missing," Hermes reasoned. He quickly herded the remaining cattle into a cave and rushed home to his gently swaying cradle.

Soon, however, the silence was broken by the angry shouts

of his stepbrother Apollo, the sun god. The cattle Hermes had taken belonged to Apollo. Hermes again climbed out of his cradle, this time to apologize to Apollo. He promised to return the cattle and, as a peace offering, gave Apollo his new lyre. Apollo was so overwhelmed by his brother's gift that he forgot his anger and gave Hermes a magic wand.

With his new toy in hand, the young Hermes ran out of the house and into a field, where he saw two serpents fighting. He thrust his wand between the two snakes, and they immediately wrapped themselves around the wand. "This will be my symbol," Hermes thought, and so it has remained throughout history.

Zeus was so proud of his infant son's adventurous nature and inventive spirit that he entrusted to Hermes one of Mount Olympos' most important positions, messenger of the gods. Legend says that Zeus gave his son winged sandals and a broad-brimmed winged hat to help him perform his new duties.

Since Hermes traveled through many lands, the ancients regarded him as the patron of all travelers. He is thought to have been the first to suggest signposts at crossroads as a convenience for travelers. When the ancients designed these posts, they felt that a four-sided pillar would be best, as the number four was sacred to Hermes, who had been born in the fourth month.

The Greeks who first used these pillars called them hermae *and often used them as milestones. On some were written riddles and inscriptions honoring war heroes.*

The ancients also considered Hermes the intermediary between the world of the living and that of the dead. Just as he guided the living on their journeys, he led the souls of the dead to their final resting place in the underworld. It became the custom in ancient times to place hermae on the graves of loved ones, similar to our tombstones.

HIGHLIGHT

Mercury in Today's World

Zeus' choice of a messenger was a wise one. Hermes, better known today by his Roman name, Mercury, and his symbols have flown across the centuries, linking the past and present. Mercury still delivers messages, albeit symbolically, for Western Union and FTD (Florist Transworld Delivery).

Astronomers used his name for the planet that moves so rapidly in relation to the other objects in the sky. Scientists used the wily god's name for quicksilver, the silvery substance used in thermometers, since it could move rapidly from one place to another.

Doctors remembered Mercury's trick with the snakes and chose as their symbol two snakes wrapped around a wand. This symbol bears the same name today as it did in ancient times—the caduceus. Snakes were an appropriate choice because the snake is the one animal that periodically sheds its old skin for a new one—a feat many people and doctors would love to duplicate.

Etymologists enjoy inventing words, especially words with hidden meanings, such as mercurial, a term used to express a pleasing but quite inexplicable fickleness in a person's temperament. Only when one knows the details of Mercury's life does this English adjective's descriptive meaning become clear.

The God Apollo

APOLLO AT DELOS

Legend tells us that if you dive under the small island of Delos in the Aegean Sea, you will find the enormous unbreakable chains that Zeus attached there thousands of years ago.

According to tradition, in early times, Poseidon, the god of the sea, created Delos by lifting land from the ocean's floor and placing it on the surface of the waters with his trident. As a result, this island floated throughout the Aegean Sea.

Years later, when Leto was about to give birth to Zeus' son Apollo and daughter Artemis, Zeus' wife, Hera, was so angered that she forbade any land on earth to shelter Leto.

Leto wandered from country to country seeking a place to rest. Exhausted and thirsty, Leto finally sat down beside a beautiful pond.

As she bent to drink of the cool, refreshing water, she noticed several workers who had been cutting the grass near the pond approaching her. Before Leto tasted one drop of the cold water, they began throwing muck into the pond and stirring up the water. In vain, she pleaded with them to stop.

When she could no longer bear the frustration, she raised her arms to the heavens and cried, "May you horrible men live forever in that pool!" Zeus heard her plea and acted. The men's bodies and hands turned green, their heads flattened, and their words changed to croaking sounds. Zeus had created a new

species of animals, frogs, which spend their lives jumping about in muddied pools.

But Leto's troubles were far from over. She desperately needed to rest. According to some legends, Hera, in her determination to prevent the births, constantly harassed Leto. She even sent a horrible serpent in pursuit of Leto. Other legends tell of this monster plaguing Leto and her twins after the births.

Finally, the floating island of Delos agreed to grant Leto a home if she promised that her children would never ridicule the tiny island. Leto quickly agreed. Zeus, in appreciation of Delos' hospitality, fastened the island to the ocean's floor with unbreakable chains. Never again would Delos be tossed about by wind and waves.

The day for the births arrived. All the gods and goddesses except Hera approached the island. Hera was not about to yield. By devious means, she concealed Eileithyia, the goddess of childbirth. Leto suffered for nine days and nights, until the assembled deities could no longer endure her pain. They dispatched Iris, the messenger goddess, to Olympos to fetch Eileithyia. Once Eileithyia arrived, the twins Apollo and Artemis were born.

How Delos rejoiced! Golden flowers burst into bloom. The gods and goddesses bathed the infants and fed them their heavenly food—ambrosia and nectar. After tasting this divine food, Apollo stood up and announced to all that he would henceforth be his father's messenger and would reveal to all humans the will of Zeus.

As the spokesman for the king of the gods, Apollo became the god of prophecy. Because of Apollo's legendary ability to predict the future, the Greeks worshiped him as the god of light and the god of civilization. Numerous temples throughout the ancient world were dedicated to him. One of the greatest sanctuaries of Apollo was located at Delos, his birthplace.

APOLLO AT DELPHI

Legend says that Apollo traveled throughout Greece until he arrived in Boeotia in the eastern part of Greece. There, as he was about to lay the foundations of the temple, the nymph of the nearby stream advised him to go elsewhere. She told him that the constant noise of horses and mules quenching their thirst in the stream had robbed the area of the silence needed for an oracular site (a place where one foretold the future). The nymph gave Apollo this advice because she feared that she would be forgotten if the great god built his temple near her stream.

Unaware of her motives, Apollo proceeded to Crisa, near Mount Parnassos in central Greece, as the nymph had advised. The lush green hills, magnificent vistas, and quiet solitude of the area appealed to Apollo.

Yet all did not proceed smoothly. A horrible serpent had been destroying the countryside. (Some sources say that this was the same monster that had chased Apollo's mother, Leto.) After a dreadful fight, Apollo slew the serpent with golden arrows. Placing his foot on the dying monster, he cried, "Now rot!" (using the Greek verb *puthein*, meaning "to rot"). Thereafter, the creature was

APOLLO DOVE INTO THE SEA, CHANGED HIMSELF INTO A DOLPHIN, AND JUMPED ABOARD THE SHIP. STARTLED AND FRIGHTENED, THE CREW WATCHED IN AMAZEMENT AS THE SHIP, WITH THIS INCREDIBLE DOLPHIN AT THE HELM, SEEMED TO STEER ITS OWN COURSE.

known as the Python or Pytho, the games celebrated every four years in joyous commemoration of this great victory were called the Pythian games, and Apollo's special priestess was named the Pythia.

Apollo still needed priests. As he looked out over the sea from his temple, he saw sailing to the south a ship from the Mediterranean island of Crete. Apollo dove into the sea, changed himself into a dolphin, and jumped aboard the ship. Startled and frightened, the crew watched in amazement as the ship, with this incredible dolphin at the helm, seemed to steer its own course. Soon the vessel entered the bay of Crisa.

Suddenly, the strange dolphin lifted up toward the sky and turned into a blazing star. Before the crew members could regain their senses, Apollo approached them dressed as a young man. Calmly, he asked who they were. Eager for information about the area, they in turn questioned him. Apollo then revealed himself as a god and invited them to become the priests of his new temple. Because he had appeared to them first as a dolphin (*delphis*, in Greek), he requested that they call him Apollo Delphinios. Legend also says that the name Crisa was changed to Delphi for the same reason.

rtemis: The Goddess of the Hunt

The Greek goddess Artemis was patroness of the hunt, the moon, youth, and wild beasts. Throughout the Greek world, ardent followers proclaimed her virtues and offered sacrifices at her favorite spots. Her origin, however, remains a mystery.

That the name Artemis is not Greek suggests that the worship of Artemis predated Greek civilization on the mainland. Many authorities suggest that her worship began in the East, where the Ephesians* regarded her as the mother goddess.

So entrenched was her worship that subsequent generations did not abandon her temples. Rather, the Greek practices surrounding the worship of a similar goddess were gradually combined with those of the Ephesian Artemis. The inhabitants of the East, especially those of Ephesos, continued to revere Artemis as the mother goddess. The mainland Greeks gradually came to associate Artemis with Apollo, the sun god.

According to classical Greek mythology, Artemis was Apollo's twin sister. Apollo represented the sun and its dazzling, golden radiance, while Artemis represented the chaste, silver brilliance of the moon. Apollo was the prince of archery, Artemis the huntress, with the slender

**The Ephesians were the inhabitants of Ephesos, a Greek city in western Asia Minor (present-day Turkey).*

arc of the moon her bow and its beams her arrows. That the Greeks worshiped her also as the patroness of youth and the young may have resulted from her early association with the Ephesian Artemis.

The Greek Artemis did not care for love. Rather, she dedicated herself to the forest and woods. "Love is a weakness, a frailty not to be allowed," Artemis told her followers. Few temples were built in her honor. Instead, hunters and worshipers laid their offerings—antlers, skins, and edible portions of deer and other animals—on rustic altars in woodland chapels.

The Romans later adopted the characteristics of the Greek Artemis and combined them with the characteristics of open air and open country associated with their goddess of the moon, Diana. Each goddess retained a few unique characteristics, however. For instance, Artemis' temples were adorned with stags' horns and Diana's with cows' horns.

This kindly maiden goddess was not without a temper. Should a follower disagree or disregard her wishes, she could become quite vengeful. She also possessed human feelings. If one of her followers suffered unjustly or too much, she quickly intervened to rectify the situation.

Athena: The Goddess of Athens

Zeus' first wife was his cousin, the goddess Metis. Since Metis was the granddaughter of Kronos, she was considered a Titan. But it was Metis who wisely advised Zeus to add mustard and salt to Kronos' nectar, the fateful concoction that caused him to vomit the children he had swallowed.

When Metis and Zeus were joyfully preparing for the birth of their first child, the wise old goddess of the earth, Gaia, came to visit her grandson Zeus. "Be forewarned, my dear Zeus. If Metis is allowed to bear two children, your fate will be the same as your father's and your grandfather's. This time she carries a girl, but next time it will be a boy who will dethrone you and become king of the gods."

Zeus listened and then panicked as had his father and grandfather. When he regained control of himself, he formed a clever plan. That evening, when he and Metis were discussing the day's events, she noticed that he was kinder and gentler than usual. Suddenly, however, Zeus opened his mouth as wide as he could, grabbed Metis, and swallowed her, child and all. Zeus' worries were over. The threat was gone.

Years later, when Zeus had all but forgotten the incident, his head began to throb uncontrollably. His screams could be heard throughout the world. The

"CUT OPEN MY FOREHEAD AND LET THE CREATURE OUT! NOW!" HEPHAESTOS DID NOT HESITATE. WITH A MIGHTY SWING, HE SPLIT OPEN ZEUS' HEAD. OUT JUMPED A FULL-GROWN GODDESS ARMED WITH A SHIELD, HELMET, AND BREASTPLATE.

Olympians came to offer their help, but not one of them had any ideas as to the source of the pain or a remedy for it. When Hermes returned to Olympos after delivering a message, he remembered how Zeus had treated Metis and immediately knew the cause of the pain.

Hermes reminded Zeus of the incident: "Zeus, within your head is the child Metis was carrying when you swallowed her." Zeus believed him, as the pain was so severe that he could not argue or even think.

Hermes ran to find Hephaestos, the god of fire, and persuaded his fellow Olympian to fetch his ax and hurry to Zeus' palace. When the two returned to the chambers of the mighty god, Zeus sat down and offered Hephaestos his head. "Cut open my forehead and let the creature out! Now!"

Hephaestos did not hesitate. With a mighty swing, he split open Zeus' head. Out jumped a full-grown goddess armed with a shield, helmet, and breastplate. Zeus and the Olympians named her Athena. Because she had sprung directly from Zeus' head, she was worshiped as the goddess of wisdom.

Athena also was revered as the preserver of the state and the protector of civilized life. As the guardian of the state, Athena was considered the goddess of war. It is said that in combat, Athena wisely kept soldiers from wanton, unnecessary slaughter.

As her special area, Athena chose Attica, in central Greece. Poseidon, the god of the sea, also coveted this area. Hence, the gods decided that a contest should be held. Whoever produced that which could be considered more beneficial to Attica would be declared the winner.

Athena and Poseidon met on the Acropolis. Some sources say that the people of Attica were the judges; others believed that the winner was decided by the gods. In any event, after all had assembled, the contest began. Poseidon struck a rock, and instantly a salt spring gushed forth. (Some sources say the first horse ever seen leaped out of the rock.) Athena then touched her spear to the ground and brought forth a noble tree laden with glossy black fruit. She named it the olive tree.

Without hesitating, the gods proclaimed Athena the victor, for surely this tree would regenerate itself and produce quantities of edible and marketable fruit, oil, and fine wood. The choice was an excellent one, for the olive tree has always been one of the mainstays of Greek agriculture.

In appreciation for Athena's gift, the people of Attica named their chief city Athens and built on the Acropolis a magnificent temple that they called the Parthenon in her honor. (*Parthenos* means "maiden," and according to Greek mythology, Zeus and the gods had decreed that Athena was to remain single.) The sculptured scenes adorning the temple immortalized Athena's birth, her victory over Poseidon, and the homage paid her by the Athenians during the Panathenaic Festival.

Within this beautiful edifice the renowned sculptor Phidias placed a colossal thirty-foot statue of the goddess clothed in an ankle-length robe of gold. The statue's face had a thoughtful, earnest expression that added to the figure's overall majesty. Because Athena was born of a god, not a goddess, Phidias' statue more closely resembled the figure of a male. The face, hands, and feet were of ivory and the eyes of precious stones. An intricately worked, massive shield stood by her feet. Her right hand held a lance, while her left supported a six-foot statue of Nike, the goddess of victory. A beautifully ornamented helmet was positioned on her head, and on her chest lay the aegis, the indestructible shield that Hephaestos had fashioned for Zeus.

Under the divine protection of Athena, the city-state of Athens prospered and became the most powerful and influential of all the Greek city-states.

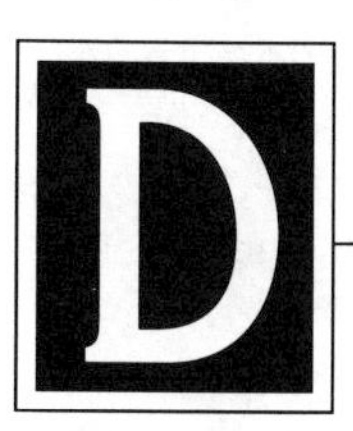

ionysos' Birth

In very ancient times, a Greek legendary hero named Kadmos founded the city of Thebes, in eastern Greece. His daughter Semele was the most beautiful of all his children. Even Zeus had noticed her beauty. One day when Hera, his wife at this time, left on some errand, Zeus took advantage of her absence to visit Semele.

Zeus left all his royal clothes, weapons, and gear at the palace, but he did not disguise himself. He approached the orchard where Semele was picking fruit and asked to visit with her. He told her that he was Zeus, and she believed him. He even promised her that if she ever had one wish, he would grant it. In the months that followed, they spent many happy hours together, until jealous Hera began to sense that something was amiss.

When Hera learned that Semele was to bear Zeus' child, she was furious. She fumed in her chambers high on Mount Olympos, where she formed a wicked plan. She went to Thebes and entered the royal palace disguised as Semele's old nursemaid.

"My dear, sweet Semele, I must advise you," Hera said.

"Please do, my nurse, for I shall do whatever you suggest," Semele replied.

"My child, I know you say and believe that Zeus is the father of your soon-to-be-born child, but many men lie about themselves. You must make him prove he is Zeus. Ask him to come to you dressed as he does to visit the gods and goddesses. If he returns, you will know he is Zeus."

"Yes," Semele thought, "surely that is good advice."

The next day Zeus came to Thebes to visit Semele. "Zeus, do you remember your promise of long, long ago when you said you would grant whatever I asked?" Semele inquired.

"Yes, my dear, I remember," Zeus replied. "What is it you desire?"

"Mighty Zeus, I wish that you would visit me not as a simply dressed god, but in the clothes

NO OTHER GREEK OR ROMAN GOD AFFECTED THE LIVES AND PRACTICES OF HIS FOLLOWERS AS DID DIONYSOS.

and gear that you use when you meet with Hera and the other Olympians."

"Please, my innocent child," pleaded Zeus, "do not ask such a favor. You do not understand."

"You promised!" Semele retorted. She was adamant, and Zeus could not go back on his word. With a very heavy heart, he returned to Mount Olympos, opened the doors of his dressing room, and slowly and sadly began to dress. He donned his brilliant cloak of lightning. He lifted the massive thunderbolts, leaving behind the greatest of them, threw the cape of storm clouds over his shoulders, and headed back to Thebes.

Semele, meanwhile, was quite anxious. If he did not return, he was not Zeus. If he did, how would he appear? She was never to know, for as Zeus entered her chambers, the brilliance of his attire and the heat of his weapons destroyed Semele. Zeus stood at the door, deeply grieved at what he had been powerless to prevent.

Hermes, the messenger god, had been aware of the unfolding tragedy and swiftly entered the room, bent down over the charred remains of Semele, and took the unborn baby from its mother's womb. Quickly, he made a cut in Zeus' thigh and carefully placed the baby inside. Just as quickly, he sewed the cut closed with special golden thread.

For three months, the baby matured inside Zeus' thigh, absorbing Zeus' immortal and godly nature. Then, at the proper time, Zeus and Hermes carefully removed the stitches and separated the skin along the cut, giving birth to the god Dionysos.

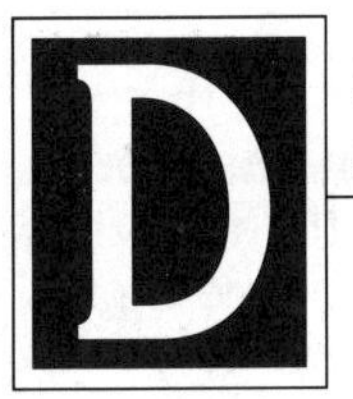

Dionysos and His Followers

No other Greek or Roman god affected the lives and practices of his followers as did Dionysos, also known to the Greeks as Bakchos and to the Romans as Bacchus and Liber. The son of Zeus, Dionysos was the only Olympian deity to have been born a mortal.

Zeus entrusted Dionysos to the nymphs of Nysa, a mountain of legendary fame. Zeus placed Silenos, the son of the woodland god Pan, in charge of Dionysos' education. This potbellied, jovial old man was the oldest of a group of woodland spirits known as satyrs, whose pug noses, bristling hair, goatlike ears, and short tails made them a favorite subject of ancient artists. From all accounts, Silenos was no disciplinarian, as his fondness for wine usually clouded his mind and thoughts. Representations of him usually portray him carrying an empty wineskin and sitting astride a donkey, as he could not trust his wobbly legs.

Dionysos soon discovered for himself the nature of the vine and a method of extracting its

WHOEVER GLADLY AND WILLINGLY WELCOMED DIONYSOS AND HIS FRIENDS RECEIVED THE GIFT OF WINE; THOSE WHO RESISTED HIS ENTRY INTO THEIR TERRITORY WERE PUNISHED SEVERELY.

juices. Not content to keep this find to himself and his followers, Dionysos undertook the task of spreading cultivation of the vine and its use. He also promoted the worship of himself as the god of wine and vegetation. Everywhere he went, nymphs, satyrs, and other woodland deities followed him. Whoever gladly and willingly welcomed Dionysos and his friends received the gift of wine; those who resisted his entry into their territory were punished severely. Many are the myths the ancients recounted of his travels.

Once, when visiting the islands of the Aegean, young Dionysos was mistaken by some pirates for a mortal. The pirates, thinking him to be the son of a noble, kidnapped Dionysos, brought him aboard their ship anchored in the harbor, and confined him below. Some of the crew thought that a demand for ransom should be made; others suggested that he be sold in Egypt. The pilot of the pirate ship sensed something different about the new captive and asked Dionysos to pardon him for the violence done him. When the other pirates heard the pilot's plea, they scorned and ridiculed him as a madman.

"Do not worry," one of them then said to Dionysos. "We mean you no harm and will take you where you will."

"To the island of Naxos then," replied the young god.

All was well until the god of wine realized that the ship was continuing south and had not veered toward Naxos. Yet Dionysos still did not reveal himself. Instead, he began to weep. The pirates laughed and scoffed at his fear and lack of bravery.

Suddenly, the ship stopped midway between the waves. In vain, the oarsmen tried to row and the mariners tried to set more sail. As all sought the reason for the boat's paralyzed state, a vine laden with great clusters of grapes spread in all directions up and along the mast and sails. Green ivy entwined itself around the mast, beautiful fruit burst forth, and fragrant wine flowed throughout the ship. The pirates stood motionless until the captain regained his senses and ordered the pilot to head to the nearest land.

Before the pilot could react, the young god changed himself into a fierce, roaring lion and caused an enormous shaggy bear to appear on deck. Pandemonium reigned. No one knew what to do. Recalling that the pilot had earlier befriended Dionysos, the pirates rushed to his side at the stern and stood around him.

Without warning, the lion leaped to the stern and seized the pilot. In a panic, the other crew members sought to escape the paralyzed ship and the monstrous beasts by leaping into the sea. But Dionysos was determined to punish them. As each pirate dove into the sea, Dionysos turned him into a dolphin. Only the pilot remained on board, for the lion held him so tightly that he could not escape.

Once the crew had been punished, Dionysos assumed his youthful figure and addressed the pilot: "Fear not, my friend. I am Dionysos, the god of wine. I do not wish to harm you, only to thank you for your kind words when I was imprisoned. Now I seek your aid in steering this vessel toward the island of

Naxos." The pilot eagerly agreed to Dionysos' request, then made his own—that he be allowed to accompany the god on his travels.

Exploits such as this won Dionysos many followers. As he traveled throughout the ancient world and his association with wine and merriment became known, great festivals were held in his honor. His female followers, called Mainades,* carried staffs decorated with ivy and topped with a pine cone. On certain occasions, they were said to wander at night through woods and mountains, fawn skins flung over their shoulders, their heads thrown back, their flying locks crowned with ivy or snakes. As they waved wands and torches, accompanied by the hollow sound of the drum and the shrill notes of the flute, they danced wildly and made insane cries of jubilation.

Although these rites were often banned, the followers of Dionysos found a way to continue their practices. Dionysos, his head crowned with vine leaves or wreaths of ivy, and the festive Mainades were favored subjects of the ancient artists. They remain so today, as their dancing figures grace vases, theater lobbies, and the internationally acclaimed designs on English Wedgwood jewelry and china.

These women are known by a number of Greek and Roman names.

Kalliope and Her Sisters

Kalliope and her eight sisters, known as the Muses, were born to Zeus and the goddess of memory, Mnemosyne, on the northern slope of Mount Olympos. Kalliope was considered their leader. These goddesses of poetry, dance, music, the sciences, and learning in general received from Zeus and Mnemosyne all that was needed to create works of art. They sang and played at the weddings and festivals of the gods, judged musical contests, and helped make mankind happy with their music.

The ancients erected few temples to the Muses, but poets and writers always prayed to them for divine inspiration, a custom that exists even today. The temples that were built in honor of the Muses and dedicated to learning were known as museums. Today this word refers to buildings where objects related to the arts and sciences are preserved for us.

Kalliope and her sisters spent most of their time playing, dancing, and writing at the foot of Mount Olympos and on nearby Mount Pieros, where they frequently met Apollo, the god of the sun and of music. It is said that Apollo learned the art of music and song from the Muses.

"KALLIOPE" IS A COMBINATION OF TWO GREEK WORDS MEANING "BEAUTIFUL VOICE."

On Mount Helikon and Mount Parnassos, both in Greece, the nine sisters led choral dances in honor of Apollo. Kalliope fell in love with Apollo. Their son, Orpheus, inherited his parents' ability to sing and to write.

Athena, the goddess of wisdom, gave the Muses the delightful winged horse Pegasos as a companion. With his hoof, Pegasos created the spring and fountain of Hippocrene on Mount Helikon so that the Muses could rest by its cool waters.

One of the many interesting stories about the Muses involved King Pieros of Thessaly, an area in northern Greece. King Pieros had nine daughters whom he loved dearly. Since he also thought very highly of the Muses, he named each daughter after one of them. These girls dared to challenge the Muses to a singing contest. Because they were mortals, the daughters of Pieros lost the contest. As a consequence of their boldness, they were changed into magpies, birds that are known for their constant chirping.

The Muses had beautiful voices. In fact, the name "Kalliope" is a combination of two Greek words meaning "beautiful voice." It is sad that this name is used today for the instrument that plays the high-pitched music we associate with merry-go-rounds and circuses.

The term "music" also comes from the name of these goddesses. In ancient times, recitations and dramatic performances were accompanied by singing or instruments. Because the Muses were the patronesses of the arts, the accompanying sound was called music.

HIGHLIGHT

Kalliope's 'Epic' Legacy

In very ancient times, Greek poetry was connected with the worship of the gods. Gradually, poets began to emphasize the myths that had developed regarding the births, deeds, and sufferings of their deities. Since the majority of people were unable to read or write, however, the poets spoke rather than wrote their compositions, usually to the accompaniment of a lyre.

As each generation passed its works and thoughts to the next, the stories grew in length. The authors no longer confined themselves to the actions of the gods on Mount Olympos, but they also began to incorporate the deeds of the great legendary heroes into their poems. To name this type of narrative poem, which celebrated the achievements of a mythical or historical hero or heroes, the Greeks used their word *epos*, meaning "a narrative" or "a song." In English, we term this style of writing "epic."

Around the eighth century B.C., the Greek poet Homer wrote the *Iliad* and the *Odyssey,* which are considered unequaled masterpieces of epic literature. Publius Virgilius Maro (70–19 B.C.), the author of the Roman epic the *Aeneid,* readily admitted his dependence on Homer's works.

The Romans were not the only imitators of the epic style. The English writer John Milton (1608–1674) patterned his *Paradise Lost* after Virgil's *Aeneid*. The English novelist Henry Fielding (1707–1754) closely paralleled Homer's *Odyssey* when he wrote *Tom Jones*. Other nations also realized that a national epic helped create or reveal a common heritage and served to instill a stronger sense of patriotism in the citizens of that country. Throughout the Western world, various stories of epic proportion have been compiled: the English *Beowulf,* the French *The Song of Roland,* the German *Nibelungenlied,* the Portuguese *The Lusiads,* and the Spanish *El Cid.*

HEPHAESTOS: THE GOD OF FIRE

1. What role did Hera play among the Olympians?
2. How did Hephaestos repay his mother for her cruel treatment of him?
3. Why was Dionysos and not Ares able to persuade Hephaestos to loosen Hera's bonds?
4. What does the myth of Hephaestos tell about the personalities of the Olympians?
5. Why do you think the ancients created a myth in which Hephaestos preferred living on earth to living on Mount Olympos?

THE INVENTIVE HERMES

1. How did Hermes appease his stepbrother Apollo after stealing his cows?
2. Why did doctors take Mercury's caduceus as their symbol?
3. What is the significance of Hermes' leaving his cradle to begin his adventures?
4. Hermes played a role in many ancient myths. Why do you think this was so?
5. In ancient times, thieves honored Hermes as their patron god. Why?

THE GOD APOLLO/ ARTEMIS: THE GODDESS OF THE HUNT

1. How did Hera harass Leto?
2. What areas of ancient life did Artemis protect?
3. Why did Apollo need priests for his temple?
4. How do the traits of Apollo and Artemis complement one another?
5. Myths of the birth of Apollo and Artemis involve several gods and goddesses as well as humans. Why did Apollo and Artemis interact so much with other gods and goddesses and with humans?

ATHENA: THE GODDESS OF ATHENS

1. What was Gaia's prophecy, and how did Zeus plan to prevent it from coming true?
2. In her contest with Poseidon, what was Athena's gift to Athens? Why was her gift better than Poseidon's?
3. What reasoning could Hermes have used when he summoned Hephaestos to help Zeus?
4. Athena was worshiped as the goddess of wisdom. Why did the Greeks have her spring from her father's head in full armor?
5. How did Phidias' statue of Athena reflect the Greeks' beliefs about her?

DIONYSOS' BIRTH/ DIONYSOS AND HIS FOLLOWERS

1. Why did Zeus not want to appear before Semele dressed in his Olympian finery?
2. Why did pirates kidnap Dionysos? Which pirate befriended him?
3. What fault did Semele possess?
4. What was the significance of having vines and ivy paralyze the pirate ship?
5. Why are the rites and rituals associated with Dionysos often uncontrolled and full of merriment?

QUESTIONS FOR DISCUSSION

1. Animals are often involved in myths about the Olympians. Review the myths in this chapter. For each one, list the animals, the gods and/or goddesses, and the particular incident involved.
2. Male and female deities in Greek and Roman mythology often complement each other. Give specific examples of this trait in the stories included in this chapter.

SUGGESTED ACTIVITY

Zeus and Hera had many children not mentioned in this chapter. Find out who they were and the areas and activities they patronized.

ADVENTURES OF THE GODS

The Master Spinner

Many techniques, tools, and machines trace their roots not to one individual, but to a great variety of improvements and modifications made over a number of years. While the ancients recognized this fact, they also believed that the traits of inventiveness and creativity were given to humans by the gods. According to the Greeks and Romans, the tragic myth of a famed weaver named Arachne clearly illustrated what happened to a creative individual who refused to thank the gods for blessing her with such skill.

Long, long ago in Asia Minor (present-day Turkey), in the area known as Lydia, there lived a renowned dyer named Idmon and his beautiful daughter Arachne. Idmon's specialty was purple dye, the color used to highlight and adorn the clothes of kings and leaders. Since the best purple was obtained by using the tiny bladders of two Mediterranean sea animals—the trumpet shell snail and the purple shell snail—it was scarce. Hence, purple-dyed clothes were very expensive.

As soon as Arachne could help, Idmon allowed her to work with him in his studio. She was a model pupil and quickly learned the art of dyeing and, in time, the art of weaving. At a very young age, Arachne became known as a master weaver. Unfortunately, Arachne was very proud and haughty. "Surely I can outweave Athena, the goddess of weaving, or any god or goddess on Mount Olympos," she boasted one day.

Since such comments did not go unheard on Mount Olympos,

Athena decided to visit the conceited Arachne, but she did not wish to reproach the girl immediately. "I shall give her a chance to see how foolishly she is behaving," Athena said. So she disguised herself as an old woman and set off for Idmon's studio. It was easy to find, since lines of people stood before it waiting for a chance to see the masterpieces created by Arachne. Athena stood in line, too. When she passed Arachne working on her loom, the disguised goddess bent over and whispered in her ear, "Listen to me, an old woman experienced in the ways of the world. Do not be so proud. Do not think yourself better than the gods on Mount Olympos, for it was they who endowed you with the ability to weave."

The foolish girl laughed aloud as she tossed her head to one side and looked directly at the old woman. "I cannot help but boast," she said. "No one is better than I, not even Athena. Hear my words: O great Athena, I challenge you to a weaving contest!"

With that, she prepared to turn away from the woman, but the sight before her eyes made her stop and stand very still. "Where is the old woman?" she asked. "And who are you?"

The woman replied, "I am Athena, the goddess you just challenged." Arachne paled, her heart beating irregularly. What could she do now?

"Oh, how foolish I have been!" she thought to herself. But then she thought, "No! I can outweave Athena. I gave my word, and I shall prove it!" Speaking aloud, she said, "Athena, let the contest begin."

Two looms were set up. The contestants sat down, each prepared to do her best. Arachne defiantly chose her theme—the wrongdoings of the gods and goddesses on Mount Olympos. Carefully and skillfully she wove. Royal purple was the predominant color. "Surely no one can weave better than this," Arachne thought as she finished.

Athena, meanwhile, forgot Arachne and thought of an appropriate theme for her piece. For the central motif, she chose the contest between herself and the sea god Poseidon for the city of Athens. In each of the corners, Athena depicted a tale in which a mortal had struggled against an immortal and lost.

When Athena finished her masterpiece, she stood up from the loom and walked toward Arachne. Anger overwhelmed her as she saw the perfect workmanship of her rival. Athena could not control herself. "You presumptuous girl," screamed the envious goddess as she destroyed Arachne's design.

Arachne lowered her head and left the room. "Death surely would be better than life after such a humiliating defeat!" she whispered, unaware that Athena was following right in her footsteps.

"Death!" cried Athena. "Absolutely not! You must live as an example of what happens to anyone who spurns the gods who endowed all humans with their talents. You and your descendants shall live by the loom that destroyed you. Henceforth, when mortals gaze upon you and admire your skill, they shall remember that your ability to produce such work comes from us, the gods and goddesses on Mount Olympos."

Athena took a vial filled with magic juices from her pocket and poured the contents over Arachne. Slowly, the girl's head began to shrink; her eyes, nose, and ears fell off; her body grew smaller and smaller; her fingers and toes attached themselves to her sides and became her legs. When she finally dared to look down at her body, she saw a fine "thread" being produced from her stomach area. As she took her first awkward steps with her eight new legs, she realized that she had become a "loom" whose thread would travel with her forever.

In ancient times and throughout the centuries, spiders and their webs have continued to inspire weavers, designers, and crafts-people in all media. The ancient Greeks used the name Arachne to identify the invertebrate she had become: a spider. In English, we use her name to form arachnid, the term denoting the class of invertebrates that includes spiders.

FAR TO THE WEST, IN THE LANDS OF HESPERIA, THERE STOOD A MARVELOUS TREE. ITS FRUIT WAS GOLDEN, AND SO WERE ITS LEAVES.

Maidens of the West

Far to the west, in the lands of Hesperia,* there stood a marvelous tree. Its fruit was golden, and so were its leaves. The great goddess Earth had presented it to Hera on the occasion of her marriage to the king of the gods, Zeus. Hera so loved the tree that she begged Earth to plant it in her special garden to the west, near Mount Atlas, in Libya. Whenever possible, the queen of the gods would leave her lofty home on Mount Olympos and travel many miles to her wondrous garden. There she would sit admiring her prized possession—Earth's beautiful tree with its golden apples.

"Suppose someone should find his way to my garden and destroy my tree and its fruit," Hera thought. "No! I must not even think of such a disaster! But it could happen, and I must be prepared." Without further delay, Hera approached Atlas, a Titan to whom Zeus had given the burdensome task of carrying the world on his shoulders.

"Mighty Atlas, I wish to ask of your daughters a great favor," Hera said. "Where might I find them?" Atlas looked at the queen of the gods and smiled. He noticed how frequently she visited the western garden since the marvelous tree had been planted. He had watched her expression change from joyous to very pensive and sad as she admired each golden apple. He knew what she wished to ask.

"My dear queen," he said, "do you need my daughters to guard your great tree? If so, I can answer for them. They shall consider

**The Greeks first called Italy Hesperia. Later the Romans called the land to their west Hesperia (present-day Spain and Portugal). In general, it was the term used to designate western lands.*

"HERE, MY GOOD MAN, KNEEL ON ONE KNEE AND BEND YOUR HEAD FORWARD," ATLAS SAID. "DO NOT MOVE QUICKLY OR SHIFT POSITIONS, OR YOU WILL CAUSE MUCH HAVOC THROUGHOUT THE WORLD."

it an honor and a privilege to do so."

Hera accepted his offer. Then she left for Mount Olympos, where there was much for her to do. She was behind in her duties because she had been spending too much time in her prized garden.

Atlas' daughters were overjoyed at the request and rushed to begin their task. They were a merry group,* dancing and singing their way about the garden. Sometimes, however, they were too carefree and wandered far from the tree. On occasion, the Hesperides, as the fair maidens were called, even dared pluck some golden apples for themselves. Ever-present Rumor, the invisible goddess who had a thousand eyes and tongues, had been watching the Hesperides with great interest. She reported what she had seen to Hera, who listened attentively but gave no answer.

"What shall I do?" Hera asked. "The Hesperides certainly do enliven the garden. Even the trees and plants have been more fruitful since their arrival. I cannot punish them! But how shall I protect my wedding present? I know what I will do! I will summon a dragon, a fire-breathing dragon. Ladon! Come, please!"

Even Hera shuddered as she saw the hundred-headed Ladon approach. "Certainly, if he guards my tree, no one will dare seize an apple!" Hera thought. Then she instructed the monster: "Ladon, your task is an easy one. Stand by my tree at all times and let no one approach!"

When Rumor heard of the dragon's task, she quickly spread the tale. The garden became quiet with Ladon guarding it, until the great hero Herakles arrived on an adventurous mission.

Herakles had been advised by the priestess at the oracle of Delphi to place himself under the care of Eurystheus to atone for several of his misdeeds. Eurystheus, a great-grandson of Zeus, was the king of Mycenae, in southern Greece. For twelve years, Herakles served Eurystheus, performing incredible tasks. Herakles now faced his most difficult task: to snatch the golden apples from Hera's tree.

To learn the whereabouts of the marvelous garden, Herakles sought the help of Nereus, Earth's son and a wise old god of the sea. But Nereus refused to answer Herakles because he had promised not to disclose his mother's secret to anyone.

"But I must know!" pleaded Herakles. Nereus turned away, only to be held fast by the mighty hero. The sea god's attempts to escape were in vain. Finally he yielded, mapped out the route, and warned Herakles of the horrible monster Ladon and the ever-present dancing guardians, the "Maidens of the West."

"The Maidens of the West are the Hesperides, the daughters of Atlas," Herakles thought. "Ah, I have a plan."

Without further delay, he began his long journey to the West. But instead of going to the gardens, he traveled to Mount Atlas. There he reviewed his plan in his mind. "It must work! I cannot fail," he thought.

From the mountain, he could see the edge of the earth, and below it he spied the massive shoulder of Atlas. After carefully making his way off the earth and to the base on which Atlas stood, the brave Herakles addressed

---

**Some sources say there were three sisters, while others claim four or seven.*

the greatly burdened Titan.

"How heavy the world must be on your shoulders! How you must long to visit your daughters! Perhaps we can exchange burdens for a while. I need some golden apples from the magic tree in the garden. If you will ask your daughters for them, I will bear the world on my shoulders."

"Done," replied Atlas quickly. No one had ever made such an offer. To be free of the tremendous weight for a moment was a wish he often made. But to be free of it for as long a time as Herakles had suggested was beyond all wishing.

"Here, my good man, kneel on one knee and bend your head forward," Atlas said. "Do not move quickly or shift positions, or you will cause much havoc throughout the world." Without a backward glance, Atlas set out on his stiff and somewhat shaky legs.

The great Titan did not hurry. He intended to fetch the apples for Herakles, but he also wished to enjoy his freedom. His feet tingled as they crossed the meadows and fields; his lungs rejoiced as they breathed in fresh air; his hands reached out to touch and feel everything.

Finally, he arrived at the garden. The Hesperides stood still as they watched Atlas approach. At first they thought the aromas of the fruit and flowers had distorted their vision. But as Atlas drew closer, they realized this figure was indeed real.

"Come join us, dear father. Rejoice and sing with us," they said.

"Alas, my daughters, I cannot stay. I have exchanged places with Herakles, in return for a favor." Atlas told them of his bargain.

"Father, we will gladly give you some apples. But, please, do not bear your burden again. Return to us," the Hesperides said.

"No, my children, I cannot," Atlas replied. "Farewell."

But Atlas could not forget their pleas. He returned to his old abode and there presented Herakles with the apples. "I have done as we agreed," he said. "Now I must go. I have borne the world long enough; you may now have the honor."

"Me?" Herakles thought. "He wants me to assume his responsibility! Never! What will I do? He will not take the world, and I cannot drop it. Let me think."

"Atlas, I beg you to do one favor before you go," Herakles said. "Unless I can adjust this pad on my shoulder, I am afraid I will drop my precious burden. Here, you hold it for a moment while I adjust the cloth." Without thinking, Atlas placed the world on his shoulders.

"Good-bye, and thank you, my friend," Herakles said as he snatched the apples and quickly ran eastward to Eurystheus in Greece. Poor Atlas! He had been deceived. Yet the burden was his, and he resettled himself into his accustomed position and thought of his brief taste of freedom. Meanwhile, Herakles raced to Mycenae, where he triumphantly presented Eurystheus with the golden apples of the Hesperides.

Some sources say that Eurystheus returned the apples to Herakles, who in turn dedicated them to Athena, the Greek goddess of wisdom. Athena, realizing that these sacred apples belonged not to the world of mortals but to that of immortals, carried them back to the garden of Hera and the Hesperides.

Phaëthon's Ride

"Please leave the chariot to me, my son," Helios* said. "Your strength, though it be great, is not enough for the horses of the sun!"

Had young Phaëthon heeded the advice of his father, he would never have felt the deadly sting of Zeus' thunderbolt. But Phaëthon could still hear the cruel insults of his friend and desperately needed to prove him wrong. He took the reins of the chariot without a second thought. But as he was rising above the earth, he felt the chariot pull away from him as the fiery steeds surged uncontrollably upward.

"Whoa! Whoa!" he said. "What did my father say? Whoa! What were his instructions? Oh, why did I not listen to him?" Dazed by the sights before him, Phaëthon stood clinging to the chariot, unable to move. His thoughts wandered back to the taunts of his friend Epaphos, which had resulted in this deadly ride.

"Your father, the sun god? Not so! Your mother has lied to you. Where is your proof? You have shown me none! Good day, my boastful friend."

Phaëthon's eyes were brimming with tears as he watched Epaphos turn from him and walk home. "If my father really is the sun god, why doesn't he make it known?" Phaëthon thought. "Is he ashamed of me? Zeus is not ashamed of Epaphos; everyone knows the king of gods and men is his father!"

**Helios, the ancient god of the sun, was later identified with the god Apollo.*

Slowly and sadly, Phaëthon walked home. When he saw his mother, the beautiful nymph Klymene, he burst in upon her. "Is my father the sun god? I implore you, prove it to me!" he said.

Klymene looked at her son's anguished face and knew what had happened. "Why had the sun god not revealed himself to his son or at least left something for him to treasure?" she thought.

Quickly, she dismissed this thought and lovingly laid her hand on Phaëthon's. "Yes, my son, your father is the sun god. If you need proof, go to him yourself. His palace lies not far from here."

Without a moment's hesitation, Phaëthon kissed his mother and rushed out the door. He headed due east until he reached the royal palace, glittering with gold and bronze. Its ceilings were covered with ivory, its doors with silver. The great craftsman Hephaestos had covered the walls with images of the universe—the earth, the sea, the sky, and all the inhabitants. Phaëthon confidently entered the palace and sought the room and face that might be his father's.

Phaëthon stood still when he came to the royal chambers and saw a figure clothed in a crimson robe high on a diamond-studded throne. The brilliance of the sun god and of the many deities in attendance overwhelmed him. Here were the gods and goddesses representing the Days, Months, Years, Centuries, and Seasons.

The sun god immediately recognized his son. "My son, there is nothing to fear," Helios said. "But tell me, why have you come?"

If you are my father, give me some proof so that people will believe me," Phaëthon said.

"Come to me, my son," answered the sun god as he lay aside his dazzling crown of sunbeams. "So that you may know that I am indeed your father, I will grant whatever you ask."

Phaëthon did not need time to think. He immediately said, "To guide your chariot for one day!" This had been his secret wish for years.

"Please, do not ask that," begged the sun god. "Not even Zeus can control my steeds. The road is very dangerous. You must first climb a hill that the horses can barely make. Then you must cross the sky at such a height that even I am afraid when I look at the world so far below me. Finally, you must descend at so steep an angle that even the ocean goddess Tethys, who waits every night to receive me, fears that one day I will plunge downward uncontrollably. Remember, the heavens and the stars are not stationary but move at the same time as I. It is not a pleasant trip, for many frightful monsters, such as the beasts of the zodiac, inhabit the heavens. Please make another request, and I will not refuse, I promise you."

Phaëthon heard none of his father's pleas. His eyes were riveted on the chariot, with its axle and tires of gold, spokes of silver, and diamond-studded seat—all the work of the skilled Hephaestos. Phaëthon could scarcely wait to climb aboard. Just then, Dawn threw open the purple doors of the east, and the stars and moon prepared to rest. At the sun god's command, the Hours harnessed the snorting steeds and hitched them to the chariot.

PHAËTHON, HIS HAIR AFIRE, FELL LIKE A SHOOTING STAR INTO THE ARMS OF THE GREAT RIVER GOD ERIDANOS, WHO COOLED HIS BURNING FACE WITH HIS WATERS.

"My son, let me anoint you with this ointment so that your body will be able to endure the brightness and heat of the flames," Helios said. "And take care. Do not use the whip, but rather the reins. Follow the old wheel tracks. Do not go too high or too low, or you will burn the heavens or the earth. The middle route is the safest."

Phaëthon eagerly took the reins. The fiery horses filled the air with their neighing, snorting, and pawing at the ground. As soon as the bars in front of them were let down, the steeds charged forward and upward. For a moment they slowed, aware that something was different. They veered a bit off course, but no one tugged at the reins. Uncurbed, they disregarded all commands and ran wildly across the heavens.

Phaëthon could not control them, nor could he remember his father's instructions. Panicking, he let the reins go and held tightly to the chariot, hoping to survive the terrible race, wishing that he had heeded his father's advice. Like a ship in a storm, the chariot was yanked up and down, to the left and right.

Phaëthon's mind and body recoiled at the sight of the strange and horrible figures appearing before him in the sky—the deadly Scorpio with its hooked claws, the snorting Taurus, and the roaring Leo. The horses, oblivious to the dangers of soaring too high or too low, enjoyed their new freedom and galloped along.

At first only tall mountains felt the scorching heat of the fiery sun chariot, then even Earth felt herself being singed. Soon cities and villages everywhere were aflame. Phaëthon, too, felt the chariot glowing white-hot. The sparks, ashes, and soot from the fires below flew into the air, singeing his feet, his clothes, and his body.

The heat was so intense that it scorched and blackened the skin of the people living in Africa and turned much of northern Africa into a wasteland (the Sahara Desert). The great Nile River fled and buried its head in the desert, where it remains today. The seas ran dry, and the fish lay on the sand.

Earth herself shuddered at the sight, realizing that she also would be consumed by fire. With great difficulty, she raised her trembling hands in prayer and begged Zeus to act. "The mighty Titan Atlas, who for centuries has held me on his shoulders, can barely hold my hot and burning frame. Save me quickly, O great king," she said. But Earth could not finish because the heat was overwhelming. She sank deeper into her caverns, hoping to escape, at least for a moment, the fiery blazes everywhere.

Zeus heard Earth's plea and summoned all the gods, including the sun god, to witness the great fire. "Unless I act quickly, Earth will be destroyed," he said.

Without waiting for any comment, he climbed to his lofty tower, took a deadly thunderbolt in his right hand, and hurled it at poor Phaëthon. It shattered the chariot and scattered the spokes and wheels. Phaëthon, his hair afire, fell like a shooting star into the arms of the great river god Eridanos, who cooled his burning face with his waters.

Phaëthon's sisters, the Heliades, joined the river Eridanos in caring for their dear, dead brother. Lovingly, they buried his scorched bones and inscribed these words on his tombstone: "Here lies Phaëthon, the driver of his father's chariot; if he did not control it, he at least fell from it in great daring."

When the Heliades turned to leave, they could not move. Their grief was so intense that they stood by his tomb, weeping and lamenting his tragic death. One day they felt their limbs and bodies growing still. They looked and saw bark creeping up their legs. They were turning into poplar trees. They had become the perpetual guardians of their brother's tomb. Yet they still grieved, and as the sunlight struck the salty tears running down the bark, they hardened and turned to amber.*

The sun god was so angered at the unjust death of his son that he refused to mount the sun chariot or to control his steeds. He said, "Phaëthon did create chaos, but he did not do it willfully. Killing him was unnecessary. As for myself, I can no longer be the sun god. I must retreat from the world. Enjoy the darkness and its shadows!"

Earth again had to seek Zeus' aid. "Mighty king, I need light to survive. Please act quickly," Earth said. Zeus regretted the youth's death, but he knew all would have been lost if he had not stopped Phaëthon. Now he had to act again.

Zeus approached the sun god and asked for his pardon. Then he commanded him to mount the great chariot and ride. The sun god accepted his duty to Earth and to all life. He yoked his fiery steeds and soared up into the air. Zeus then traveled from land to land to assess and repair, wherever possible, the damage caused by Phaëthon's ride.

**Amber is a fossil resin. In ancient Rome, it was the custom for brides to wear this jewel.*

The Mighty Orion

Who was Orion? Was he Artemis' beloved? Did she really kill him? Even the ancients could not answer these questions with any certainty. Many writers, both Greek and Roman, included or at least mentioned Orion's story in their works, but their accounts do not agree. Most scholars believe that certain details were added by authors writing after the classical period (240 B.C.– C. A.D. 125), when religious unity was not as great or belief in myths as strong. Scholars also believe that many of the earlier details were omitted or confused. Our version is based on the tales most often repeated in the ancient works.

In northwestern Greece, in the land known as Boeotia, there lived a peasant farmer named Hyrieus. A kindly and honest man, widowed for several years,

"SEEK THE RAYS OF THE RISING SUN. ONLY THUS SHALL YOU RECOVER YOUR SIGHT," COMMANDED THE GODS. "BUT HOW? I CANNOT SEE," ANSWERED ORION.

he had promised to remain true to his beloved wife and never marry again.

One evening, after returning home from the fields, the lonely widower noticed three strangers slowly walking along the hot, dusty road. Thinking they must be tired and thirsty, he invited them to enter his humble hut. The faces of the wayfarers brightened as they accepted his kind offer.

After a simple meal, Hyrieus asked if the three might wish to spend the night. "My lodgings are somewhat rough, but I will share them most willingly with you," he said.

The guests looked at each other and decided not to hide their true selves any longer. Suddenly, the peasant's hut shone with a brilliance that made the startled host cover his eyes and sink to his knees. His wayfarers were not Greek countrymen, but gods who had left Mount Olympos to wander the earth among mortals. They were the mighty Zeus, the powerful Poseidon, and the swift Hermes. Hyrieus was speechless—embarrassed to think he had even attempted to entertain the gods.

"I must offer a sacrifice to them," he thought as he ran from the hut to the fields. There he found his only ox, and without a moment's hesitation, he prepared to sacrifice the great beast. While he was gone, the Olympians resolved to express their gratitude to their kindly host. When Hyrieus returned to his guests, they thanked him for his hospitality and devotion and offered to grant him one wish.

"Do I dare ask for what I truly wish to have?" Hyrieus thought. "Could they possibly grant it? To be sure, they are gods, but. . . ."

Poor Hyrieus! He could not decide. Finally, he stood before the three and hesitantly made known his greatest hope: "I wish to have a son."

Without a word, the Olympians turned and slowly walked toward the sacrificial altar. They removed the ox's hide and ordered Hyrieus to bury it immediately. Without question, the peasant readily obeyed. As the gods turned to leave, they directed the bewildered farmer to return to the burial site in ten months.

Hyrieus did as he was instructed. Never did he question his divine guests' words, nor did he doubt that they would answer his request.

Finally, the day arrived, and a nervous Hyrieus approached the mound. As he did, he noticed cracks in the dirt. Something inside was trying to break out. A handsome boy was pushing up the dirt, seeking to find the sunlight. Hyrieus' joy was boundless. "I shall name him Urion," he said.

As the years passed, Urion, whose name for some unknown reason was eventually changed to Orion, grew to be a mighty hunter and was known throughout Greece for his exploits, his gigantic size, and his handsome features.

One day he ventured to Chios, an island lying to the east of Boeotia. There Orion fell in love with the king's daughter, Merope. To win her father's approval, he performed many tasks, including clearing the island of wild beasts. All was in vain, though, for Oinopion, the king, refused to set a marriage date.

Orion could no longer contain his emotions. He attempted to seize Merope and escape, but he was unsuccessful. The stubborn Oinopion now sought vengeance. He blinded Orion and cast him on the seashore. What was Orion to do? He called the gods for help.

"Seek the rays of the rising sun. Only thus shall you recover your sight," commanded the gods.

"But how? I cannot see," answered Orion.

Just then he felt the rays of the sun on his body and stretched his hands out to sense the direction from which they came. He followed them across land and sea until he reached the volcanic island of Lemnos, in the Aegean Sea.

There he proceeded to the cave of Hephaestos, the god of fire. When the latter saw the blinded giant, he took pity on him and stopped his hammering at the forge. Hephaestos commanded Kedalion, one of his men, to be Orion's guide.

With Kedalion on his shoulders, Orion sought the rays of the rising sun. They did not have long to wait, for the goddess Dawn was preparing to cast her rosy fingers across the sky just as Kedalion turned Orion's face due east. Within minutes, the sun god gave his team of horses the command to rise into the sky. As the beams fell upon Orion's eyes, the mighty hunter felt their warmth and rejoiced when he saw the bright sunlight once again flooding the earth.

Orion thanked the gods and prepared to offer sacrifices. He could see, but he could not forget the overwhelming sense of darkness he had experienced. He decided to devote himself to the goddess of the moon and became one of Artemis' devoted followers. Her twin brother, Apollo, felt somewhat scorned and chided her about Orion's attention. Artemis paid no attention to him and continued to spend much time with Orion.

One day Apollo spied Orion swimming far from the coast. All he could see of the mighty hunter was his head bobbing on the waves. Apollo quickly fetched Artemis. "See that black spot far out to sea? Prove to me your skill with the bow and arrow and hit it," dared Apollo.

Artemis reacted immediately to his challenge and pulled an arrow from her quiver. After it left her bow, it traveled straight to its mark.

Hours later, the tide carried Orion's dead body to shore. Artemis saw her arrow, remembered her brother's taunts, and bowed her head in grief. She knew she could not ask Zeus to restore Orion's life. But somehow she had to preserve him; she would not allow him to be forgotten.

Gently, she carried his body to the heavens, where he became a constellation. There he appears as a giant with a belt, sword, lion's skin, and club. His dog, Sirius, accompanies him, and the Pleiades fly before him.

Orion was not forgotten, for the goddess of the moon slowly passes by him every night on her journey across the sky. Therefore, his immortality and fame are ensured as generation after generation continues to watch his nightly progress across the heavens.

Many classicists believe that some myths were used to explain natural phenomena—the rising of the sun, the positions of the planets, the passage of the seasons, and so on. Such is the case with Orion. The morning rising of his constellation denotes the beginning of summer because he can be seen at daybreak in the eastern sky. He grows paler

as the day progresses, until Artemis casts her moonbeams across the sky and earth and slays him. His midnight rising signals autumn, the season of harvesting grapes and making wine. At the beginning of winter, the season of stormy weather, he is visible rising late and following the chase across the heavens.

AS MEMNON AND ACHILLES FOUGHT, ZEUS WEIGHED THE FATE OF EACH ON A SCALE. AS THE SCALE CONTAINING MEMNON'S FATE SANK, ACHILLES PIERCED THE SON OF EOS WITH HIS GREAT SPEAR.

awn's Tragic Loss

For centuries every morning, before Helios' flight across the sky in his golden chariot, rosy-fingered* Dawn has spread her rays across the horizon. Upon her arrival, darkness and the shadows of the night speed on their way. Since she always enjoyed seeing the happiness the dawn of a new day brought to mortals everywhere, Eos, the Greek goddess of the dawn, eagerly anticipated her daily flight across the sky. Nevertheless, her special joy was her son Memnon, the king of Ethiopia, an African nation south of Egypt.

On the day that Memnon decided to enter the Trojan War and fight for his uncle, Priam, who ruled the kingdom of Troy in Asia Minor, Eos felt a great foreboding within her that all would not be well. Her rays barely brightened the horizon that day. Ignoring his mother's pleas to reconsider his decision, Memnon, accompanied by his warriors, marched north in hopes that his fresh forces would help end the ten-year war.

Priam received him with great honor, and all Troy rejoiced that so brave a king had joined their battle against the Greeks. Impatient for action, Memnon, dressed in the armor fashioned for him by Hephaestos, led his troops to the front lines the day after his arrival. Within a short time, Memnon's spirit rekindled that of the Trojans. The Greeks were held at bay until the mightiest of all Greeks, the hero Achilles, appeared on the battlefield.

The two great warriors engaged in a fierce and deadly combat while their countrymen watched. As they fought, Zeus weighed the fate of each on a scale. As the scale containing Memnon's fate sank, Achilles pierced the son of Eos with his great spear.

Eos, who had been watching from on high, stood motionless, unable to accept her son's fate. Once she regained her composure, she summoned the Winds** to carry his body gently through the air to the banks of the river

**"Rosy-fingered" was the standard epithet used by the Greek epic poet Homer (fl. around 700 B.C.) in the* Iliad *and the* Odyssey *to describe the goddess of the dawn, named Eos by the Greeks and Aurora by the Romans.*

***The ancient Greeks and Romans regarded the South, North, East, and West winds as divine beings.*

Aisepos, north of Troy. Later that day, after the goddess of the dawn had completed her journey across the sky, she too traveled to the Aisepos. Accompanying her were the Hours, the Olympian goddesses of order and justice, and the Pleiades, the graceful daughters of Atlas.

As Eos led the sorrowful procession, her bright colors, with which she reddened the morning skies, grew pale, and Night spread the heavens with clouds. Although all was done with great solemnity, the goddess of the dawn could not bear to look as Memnon's body was placed on the funeral pyre. Rather, she flew to Mount Olympos, where she knelt before the mighty Zeus and begged: "Although I am the least of all the gods on golden Olympos and the world has built only a few scattered temples in my honor, I come to you as a goddess. I ask nothing for myself. I have lost Memnon, who carried brave arms in vain and died young. Grant him some honor and heal the wound so deep in a mother's heart."

Zeus felt compassion for Eos and granted her wish. Suddenly, the dark ashes from Memnon's funeral pyre whirled high into the air, where they joined together into an immense mass. Eos soon saw light-feathered birds emerge from the thick cloud. They flew high into the air, divided themselves into two flocks, and warred against each other with beaks and talons until all fell fluttering down as funeral offerings to the ashes of their father, Memnon. Legend says that every year the birds, known to the ancients as the Memnonides, return and perform the same ritual in their hero's honor.

As an everlasting memorial to Eos' son, the later Greeks gave the name of Memnon to the colossal statue of black stone erected near Thebes, an Egyptian city situated on the banks of the Nile River. It was said that when the first rays of morning light fell upon the statue, a sound similar to the snapping of a harp string was heard.

In spite of all the honor paid to her son by mortals and immortals, Eos remained inconsolable. Since that fateful day, tears have flowed upon the land as she moves across the sky each day. Mortals can see her tears in the form of dewdrops glistening atop the blades of grass in fields and meadows throughout the world.

The Pleiades

"How pale the Pleiades look tonight! Can they have heard of Troy's destruction?" thought an ancient shepherd tending his flocks in Boeotia, an area in northern Greece. "But wait, there are only six stars, not seven, shining tonight."

The beautiful Pleiades had not only heard of the tragedy of

FOR FIVE YEARS, ORION PURSUED THE SEVEN SISTERS, SEEKING A RETURN OF HIS AFFECTION. FINALLY, THE PLEIADES BEGGED THE GODS ON MOUNT OLYMPOS TO INTERVENE AND END THE CHASE. ZEUS ANSWERED THEIR PLEAS.

Troy, but they had seen it—all of them except Elektra. She had left the constellation because she could not bear to see the grand city of Troy, which her own son Dardanos had founded, mercilessly burned and razed, its inhabitants killed or sold into slavery.

The lives of these seven lovely goddesses had once been so carefree. Whenever Artemis, the maiden goddess of the hunt, went on an outing, the Pleiades had accompanied her. They roamed the woodlands and meadows of the earth, content to know that the responsibility of keeping the world spinning in its orbit rested on their father Atlas' shoulders. Nor did they avoid streams or waterways, for their mother, Pleione, was an ocean nymph.

Then had come that fateful day in Boeotia when the giant hunter Orion had spied them in the fields. So deeply did Aphrodite, the goddess of love, pierce his heart with love's arrows that he forgot his devotion to Artemis and his plan to remain a bachelor. For five years, he pursued the seven sisters, seeking a return of his affection. Finally, the Pleiades begged the gods on Mount Olympos to intervene and end the chase. Zeus answered their pleas.

Suddenly, in the midst of a meadow, the sisters felt their bodies lift from the ground. "Can this be a new trick devised by our pursuer?" each wondered. Then they looked at each other and saw wings where arms and hands had been and beaks instead of noses. Smaller and smaller they shrank, and a coat of feathers covered their bodies. The sisters had become doves!* Orion stood motionless, dazed by what he saw.

That night, as he watched Artemis on her journey across the sky, he saw the seven sisters, who had been lifted into the heavens and placed among the stars. Once again, their lives were carefree. Each, in turn, bore children. One was Hermes, the messenger god, and another Dardanos, the founder of Troy and the Trojan race.

Then came the fateful day when Troy was destroyed by the Greeks. Elektra, the mother of Dardanos, chose to leave her sisters rather than witness so dreadful a sight.** That night, when the remaining sisters passed over the ruined city, the fires, destruction, and tearful inhabitants so affected the goddesses that their brightness dimmed and never returned.

Yet Maia, Alkyone, Kelaeno, Asterope, Merope, and Taygete have remained the guardians of farmers and sailors. Their dawn rising in the middle of May in the Northern Hemisphere signals the time for sowing and the beginning of the sailing season, just as their morning setting at the end of October signals the approach of the harvest and the end of the sailing season.

**The erratic movements of the Pleiades in the sky cause them to resemble doves flying about. Many scholars believe that this similarity gave rise to the myth of the Pleiades.*

***Many sources say that Merope, not Elektra, was the invisible sister. They say that she hid herself in shame after marrying a mortal.*

THE MASTER SPINNER

1. Why did Idmon become renowned as a dyer?
2. What provoked Athena to accept Arachne's challenge?
3. Why do you think Athena took the form of an old woman to visit Arachne?
4. How did Athena and Arachne let their feelings influence their choice of designs?
5. Would death have been better than being condemned to live as a spider?

MAIDENS OF THE WEST

1. Why did Hera want the Hesperides to guard her golden apples?
2. How did Herakles trick Atlas into taking the world back on his shoulders?
3. Why is the ancients' description of the goddess Rumor apt?
4. How does this myth represent Atlas' personality?
5. How would you characterize Herakles' personality traits from this myth?

PHAËTHON'S RIDE

1. What incident caused Phaëthon to want to prove he was Helios' son?
2. Why did Zeus intervene and stop Phaëthon's ride?
3. How did Helios receive his son?
4. How did the ancients use Phaëthon's ride to explain the world's topography and inhabitants?
5. How do you think the ancients came upon the idea of a sun god's chariot?

THE MIGHTY ORION

1. What was Hyrieus' secret wish? How did his guests grant it?
2. What advice did the gods give Orion after he was blinded?
3. Why did Orion believe it proper that he devote himself to Artemis?
4. Why did Artemis place Orion's dead body in the sky?
5. Why did the ancients believe that the gods on occasion disguised themselves and walked among mortals?

DAWN'S TRAGIC LOSS

1. Who made Memnon's armor, and why did he make it?
2. How did Zeus answer Eos' plea to honor her slain son, Memnon?
3. Why did the Trojans leave Memnon to battle Achilles alone?
4. Why did Eos consider herself so unimportant?
5. What does the ancients' explanation of dewdrops tell you about their philosophy of life?

QUESTIONS FOR DISCUSSION

1. In several of the tales included in this chapter, the forms into which the characters were changed have continued to interact with humans through the centuries. List these forms and explain the interactions.
2. Zeus plays a role in many myths. What roles did he play in the myths included in this chapter?

SUGGESTED ACTIVITY

If you had to plan a weaving pattern based on the tale of Orion and the Pleiades, what designs would you use in the center and the four corners?

ROMANCE AMONG THE GODS

Endymion Sleeps

Because Artemis spent much of her time leading the moon across the sky or in the woodlands away from crowds of people, and because Endymion spent most of his time sleeping, the ancients did not include these two figures in many tales. Furthermore, the details of the myths in which they do appear vary from one author to the next. Yet the tale must not be overlooked, for it allows us to see Artemis not as a spurner of love, but as one in love.

One still night, Artemis, the goddess of the moon, was serenely guiding her chariot across the sky when she saw someone whom she had never before noticed. She focused her beams on the youth, the most handsome she had ever seen. But she dared not linger because other lands were awaiting her moonbeams.

The next evening, she raced across the sky until she reached Mount Latmos* in Caria, a province in Asia Minor (present-day Turkey). So excited and anxious was she that she had some difficulty slowing her team of horses. Finally, she was able to focus her moonbeams on the mountainside. There, by the cave, lay the youth, sleeping soundly as he had been the night before. But this time she did not think of those awaiting her moonlight. After a moment's hesitation, she turned toward the earth, settled the horses, and quietly approached the sleeping youth.

"How handsome he is!" she thought as she stood gazing at him. Almost without thinking, she bent over and gently kissed him. Not daring to remain any longer, she returned to her chariot. Her mind was so confused and her emotions so spent that she let her horses guide her across the sky. She had never been in love before. In fact, she had always avoided such emotions.

The following night, she tried to concentrate on her evening's mission but could not. As she neared the sky above Asia Minor, she felt her heart quickening. She had to stop again. Every night was the same. Her duties as moon goddess no longer seemed so important. Love was an emotion not to be fought!

Unfortunately, Zeus had

**The Greek term* latmos *means "oblivion" or "forgetfulness."*

noticed her tardiness and frequent absences. He also noticed that she was looking quite pale. "How can this be?" he mused. "She's always been so healthy and carefree!"

Soon he discovered the reason for the change and was obliged to act. Yet he did not wish to be unkind. He called Endymion to his chambers and offered him eternal youth and eternal life—if he remained asleep forever. Endymion accepted, and to this day, the handsome youth sleeps near a cave on Mount Latmos. Artemis tends his flocks, making sure that no sheep or lamb is harmed and that his ewes increase in number every year.

Cupid Pierces His Own Heart

People throughout the world have told many tales of romance, but one of the best tells of the time the god of love, Cupid (Eros in Greek mythology), fell in love. The myth is believed to have been told in its complete form about A.D. 150 by the Roman writer Apuleius, who borrowed the idea from an old Greek legend and added some of his own details.

Cupid was the son of Venus, the goddess of love and beauty, and the grandson of Iupiter. The ancients pictured him as a mischievous boy with curly hair and golden wings. With him always were an invisible bow and a quiver filled with arrows that caused whomever he shot, whether god or human, to fall forever in love. Venus, as the goddess of love, frequently asked him to shoot these arrows.

It so happened that there was a king who had three daughters, one of whom, Psyche, was so lovely and charming that men and women preferred to worship her rather than Venus. They even threw flowers before her as she walked. The jealous Venus ordered Cupid to pierce Psyche's heart with an arrow that would cause her to fall in love with someone horrible.

Before leaving on his mission, Cupid visited the two fountains in his mother's garden. He filled one amber vase with sweet water from the fountain of happiness and another with bitter water from the fountain of sadness. He attached these containers to his quiver and then flew to the castle of Psyche's father.

Cupid entered Psyche's room in the middle of the night and poured a few drops of the bitter water over her lips. But just as he was about to shoot his sharp arrow, the moon cast a beam across her face. Cupid could hardly believe how beautiful she was! He stared at her so intently that when he leaned forward to see her better, he accidentally pricked himself with an arrow. Immediately, he fell in love. He quickly poured the sweet water

on her lips to destroy the effect of the bitter water.

But how was Cupid to keep her forever? She was a mortal, and he was a god. Although Cupid could not answer that question, he cast a spell over Psyche so that no one would ask to marry her.

As time passed, Psyche's sisters married members of royal families, but no one seemed to want Psyche. Her father decided to seek the help of the gods.

Psyche's father traveled to the temple of Apollo, the god of prophecy. There he consulted the priest of Apollo. However, Cupid had already asked Apollo for his help in winning Psyche. Therefore, Apollo told the unhappy king that he must dress Psyche in dark clothes and lead her to the top of a certain hill where a horrible winged serpent would come to claim her as his wife. Very reluctantly, Psyche's parents led her to the rocky cliff.

For days, Psyche sat there alone, trembling and weeping. Suddenly, she felt a gentle breeze lifting her into the air. It was Zephyrus, the mildest of all the winds. After a short trip through areas unfamiliar to Psyche, Zephyrus placed her in a bed of flowers surrounded by acres of soft green grass.

When Psyche looked around, she could hardly believe her eyes. There before her was a huge mansion with columns of gold, walls of silver, and floors inlaid with glittering precious stones. Slowly, she approached the mansion and cautiously opened the huge doors. Then she heard voices beckoning her to come in, saying that the castle was hers. As she entered the great hall, she saw before her a sumptuous dinner. She heard beautiful music but did not see anyone.

As evening approached, Psyche sensed that some man had entered the hall. She looked and looked for him. Then she heard a deep, strong voice say, "I am your husband. I will visit you every evening, but I must leave before the first sign of morning. Never must you ask or try to see me!"

Psyche spent her days caring for her beautiful home and gardens. Every evening, she anxiously awaited the return of her mysterious husband. She was happy, and she wished to tell her family of her good fortune. Although her husband begged her not to return home, he finally agreed that her sisters could come to visit.

From the west came Zephyrus, who "blew" her sisters to her. They were so jealous of her good fortune that they told Psyche that her husband must be some sort of monster. Psyche did not want to believe them, but maybe they were right.

Finally, her curiosity overwhelmed her. One night after Cupid had fallen asleep, Psyche took out an oil lamp and a sharp knife (to use if he *were* a horrible monster). As she held the lamp above his face, she saw the most handsome of men. In her excitement, a drop of hot oil from the lamp fell on his shoulder. Her husband cried out in pain. Psyche, confused and upset, fell back, accidentally pricking her finger with the arrow that lay by the bed. Thus shot with his arrow, she immediately fell in love. Cupid, however, spread his wings of golden feathers and flew away, saying, "Love cannot live where there is no trust!"

Psyche then knew that her husband was the god of love. She searched in vain for him. She told her evil sisters what had happened, and they rejoiced in her misfortune.

Cupid, meanwhile, had flown to his mother, Venus, so that she might treat the burn on his shoulder. She had already heard of her son's love for Psyche and had resolved to keep the lovers separated. While Cupid recovered, she kept his room locked.

Psyche, having lost all hope of finding Cupid, decided to offer herself to Venus as a servant. Venus gladly accepted her and treated her as a slave. In addition, Venus assigned her several extremely difficult and dangerous tasks.

The first was to sort, in one day, an enormous pile of various types of seeds. "Impossible!" Psyche thought. But Cupid still loved her, and although he was imprisoned in his room, he sent thousands of ants to help her sort the seeds. Enraged, Venus threw Psyche a crust of bread and made her sleep on the ground until morning.

The next day, Venus ordered her to fetch three tufts of golden wool from the sheep that roamed

SWOOPING DOWN, CUPID WIPED THE "SLEEP" FROM PSYCHE'S EYES, RESTORED IT TO THE BOX, AND WOKE HER WITH A TOUCH OF HIS ARROWS.

a certain riverbank. Psyche thought this would be easier than the first task, but when she saw the riverbank and the savage rams in the flock, she decided to throw herself into the river. As she looked at the dark water, she heard the calming voice of the river god advising her to wait until later in the day, when the sheep slept. Then she could easily snatch tufts of fleece from the briar bushes through which the flock had passed.

Venus' third assignment was even more difficult. She ordered Psyche to fill a bottle with water from the Styx, the river that flowed around Hades, the ancients' name for the underworld. Fierce dragons kept perpetual watch there, and the riverbanks were very steep and slimy. Again Cupid made sure his love had help. An eagle swooped low, took her bottle, filled it with the murky water, and returned it to her. Venus was enraged. She decided that the fourth mission should definitely cause Psyche's death.

Venus gave Psyche a box with orders that it be given to the queen of the underworld, Proserpina. Psyche was instructed to request that Proserpina fill it with some of her beauty. Cupid came to her aid, but Psyche's curiosity overwhelmed her. She opened the box. No beauty secrets were inside. Rather, a deep sleep flew out and enveloped her.

At about that time, Cupid had regained enough strength so that he could stretch his golden wings and fly out the window. As he searched the countryside from the air, he saw Psyche asleep in a meadow. Swooping down, he wiped the "sleep" from her eyes, restored it to the box, and woke her with a touch of his arrows.

Together, Cupid and Psyche gave Venus the box. Then they approached the king of the gods, Iupiter, and asked him for permission to marry. Iupiter agreed, but first he wished to make Psyche immortal. To become immortal, she needed to taste the food of the gods. Iupiter gave her some of their nectar to drink and ambrosia to eat.

A great marriage feast was prepared on Mount Olympus, the home of the gods. All the deities, even Venus, attended. To add to the merriment and to make the occasion more memorable, the nine Muses sang and danced to the tune of Apollo's lyre.

Daphne and Apollo

Through the forests, across the meadows, and along the streams they raced—she fleeing, he pursuing. How long could she continue this exhausting pace? Daphne felt her chest tightening and her legs stiffening with each movement. But she had to continue. She would not allow Apollo to catch her. He was so close now she could feel his breath on her neck.

What had she done to cause this? Never had she given the great sun god any indication that she wished to be with him or even to see him. As a very young maiden, she had asked the gods to allow her to remain single—a request they had earlier granted Artemis, the goddess of the hunt. All had gone well until that fateful day when Apollo glimpsed her in the fields and fell immediately in love.

Poor Apollo! Being spurned by his first love was quite an insult. How he wished he had never seen or even known Eros, the god of love! How reckless he had been to ridicule such a powerful god! Apollo had not considered that Eros, despite his size and youthful appearance, possessed some of the most powerful weapons in the world. Nor did he realize how deeply he had hurt Eros with his comments. When Apollo had seen Eros bending his bow to string it, Apollo had laughed and warned him that such weapons were meant for adults, not youngsters.

Eros resolved to punish Apollo. He took his bow and two arrows from his quiver. One arrow was golden, sharp, and glistening, while the other was blunt and lead-tipped. He shot the first straight into the sun god's heart. Apollo lost control of his emotions and fell in love with beautiful Daphne.

Eros was not finished. He then shot the second arrow into Daphne's heart. The lead tip blunted all her emotions, and she scorned every move Apollo made, even when he whispered softly to her in an attempt to calm her fears. From afar he marveled at her shining eyes, her glistening hair, and her graceful hands. He had to speak with her. "Perhaps she is unaware of how great a god I am," he thought. Again he tried to approach her. "Do not run from me. I am not an enemy. You do not realize from whom you flee. I am lord of Delphi, and Zeus is my father."

Daphne could listen no longer. She began to run. Apollo stood still for a moment in disbelief at Daphne's rejection of his plea. "I cannot lose her! She must be mine," he thought, and across the fields he raced.

Escape was impossible, for who could outdistance Apollo? When Daphne felt Apollo's breath on her shoulder, she cried out to her father, the god of the Peneios River, which Daphne saw flowing in the distance. She begged him to change her body into another form.

Hardly had she finished her plea when she felt a numbness spread over her limbs. Bark grew around her chest, her hair turned into leaves, and her arms became branches. Her swift feet changed into roots, and her head became a treetop.

Still Apollo loved her. Gently, he placed his hand on the bark and felt her heart beating underneath. "Although you will never be my bride, you will be the tree that is sacred to me. Your leaves will crown my head always, and men will use them to weave garlands for victorious athletes and generals."

Yet even this did not seem to be enough. He added, "You will be as the gods and never grow old. Your leaves shall never wither and die but will always be green and shining." Thus did Apollo speak, and the leaves of this beautiful laurel tree began to rustle as if in reply.

ZEUS CALMLY REPLIED THAT HE HAD USED THE CLOUD TO HELP KEEP THIS ANIMAL, HIS NEW CREATION, A SECRET. HERA WAS NOT TO BE DECEIVED. SHE REQUESTED THAT ZEUS GIVE HER THE COW AS A PRESENT!

Io and Zeus

According to the ancients, Zeus, the king of the gods and the husband of Hera, frequently fell in love with other women. Understandably, Hera became quite jealous whenever this happened and many times harshly punished these women.

On one occasion, Io, the daughter of the river god Inachos, attracted Zeus' attention. However, he could meet her only when Hera was sleeping. To protect himself and his love from his wife's wrath, Zeus ordered a cloud to cover the entire area where he and Io walked and talked.

Nevertheless, all did not proceed as Zeus planned. One afternoon Hera awoke earlier than usual. She noticed across the land a thick cloud that never moved. Her curiosity aroused, she quickly flew down to earth to investigate. Her movements caused the cloud to stir. Thus warned that someone was approaching, Zeus immediately changed Io into a cow. Upon seeing her husband, Hera asked him about this beautiful snow-white cow at his side. Zeus calmly replied that he had used the cloud to help keep this animal, his new creation, a secret. Hera was not to be deceived. She requested that Zeus give her the cow as a present! How could he refuse?

Hera then led the cow to a beautiful green pasture. To guard Io, Hera summoned her servant Argos, a creature with one hundred eyes. So amazing was Argos that when he slept, only two eyes were closed at any one time.

Io remained a prisoner encased in the skin of a huge animal. Sadly, she walked to the bank of her father's river. When she saw her reflection in the water, she jumped back in terror. As the tears rolled down her cheeks, she tried to call her father, but even her mooing frightened her.

Upon hearing his name, her father rose to the surface of the water. He saw only a cow! He did not recognize his daughter in her new form. Then Io thought of a plan. With her front foot, she scratched the two letters of her name in the sand. Inachos understood. How happy he was to find his lost daughter! But ever-watchful Argos quickly led Io to another pasture.

Zeus had to act. He summoned his son Hermes to help him. Disguised as a shepherd, Hermes approached Argos and began to tell him stories. Argos enjoyed being entertained, and slowly his eyes began to close. Hermes continued his storytelling, with each story longer and more soothing than the last. Finally, Argos' hundredth eye closed. Hermes then took his sword and cut off Argos' head.

Hera saw poor Argos killed. Sadly but quickly, she gathered all his beautiful eyes and, taking them to Mount Olympos, placed each one at the end of a tail feather of her favorite bird, the peacock. These "eyes," the distinguishing characteristic of the peacock, became an eternal memorial to Argos.

In her anger, Hera continued to harass Io. She sent a horsefly to torment the cow. With each sting, Io ran faster and faster, fleeing from country to country trying to find some peace. She then plunged into the sea between Italy and Greece (named thereafter the Ionian Sea). Finally, she swam across the strait separating Europe and Asia. In her memory, this strait was called the Bosporus, meaning "cow crossing."

Eventually, Io took refuge in Egypt. Zeus met her there and returned her to human form. Slowly, her coarse hairs fell from her body; her eyes and mouth grew narrower; her horns shortened and disappeared; her hoofs became hands and fingers, feet and toes. How happy Io and Zeus were! Shortly thereafter a son, named Epaphos, was born to them. According to legend, Epaphos became an Egyptian king.

The Adventure of a Bull

Europa jumped from her bed, her body trembling, her teeth chattering. She slowly looked about her but saw nothing. Had she only dreamed that two women had stood by her bed, each beckoning her to follow? Again Europa's eyes searched every section of the room. Nothing! Yet it had seemed so real. Each woman had presented strong arguments as to why Europa should follow her.

One woman had seemed quite familiar and had even said she was Europa's mother. But Europa lived in the palace with her mother and father, and her father had told her that Poseidon, the great god of the sea, was her grandfather. Still, there was something about the stately figure that seemed to indicate that a close bond did exist between the two. The other woman had made no such claim but declared that Zeus himself wanted Europa to follow her.

When the goddess of the dawn began casting her rosy fingers across the sky, Europa was still searching her room and her mind for some clue of the meaning of her night visitors. "Enough!" the restless maiden thought. "I must leave this room and forget last night."

Quickly, she washed, dressed, and ate breakfast. She kissed her parents good-bye, saying, "Until this evening, for I must spend this beautiful spring day outside in the bright sunshine." Off she raced, out the palace door, across the courtyard, and toward the meadows that bordered the sandy coastline. She did not pause for even a moment until she saw the flowering meadows. Her friends were already there, laughing and playing ball. They had not had

ACROSS THE WATER HE FLEW, HIS HOOFS BARELY SKIMMING THE MEDITERRANEAN AND AEGEAN SEAS. EUROPA SAT MOTIONLESS. WHO WAS THIS BULL FOR WHOM EVEN THE GREAT SEAS CALMED THEIR WATERS?

any mysterious night visitors.

As she entered the fields, the beauty of the flowers and the divine blend of the fragrances chased the troubling thoughts from her mind. Her eyebrows relaxed, her face softened, and her heart slowed. All seemed well once again as Europa helped her friends gather bouquets of narcissuses, hyacinths, and violets.

"Let's go for a swim," called one of the maidens, and without a moment's hesitation, all slipped off their shoes and outer garments and plunged into the fresh, cool water of the nearby river.

"Surely last night was just a dream that must be forgotten!" reasoned Europa as she floated contentedly on the calm water, unaware that she was being watched from afar. Indeed, her dream had not been meaningless, and within a few hours, her life was to change drastically.

Mighty Zeus had chanced to see the beautiful Europa and her friends that fine spring morning. Feeling his heart jump and his knees weaken at the sight of the young maiden, Zeus quickly sought something to divert his attention. His efforts were in vain, for her beauty, her carefree manner, and her happy smile seemed to be etched indelibly in his heart.

Finally, Zeus surrendered to the god of love. But he had to keep his actions secret from the jealous Hera. To do this, he disguised himself as a snow-white bull.

Slowly, he approached the meadow where Europa and her friends were picking flowers. He did not wish to frighten anyone, especially his love. He need not have been afraid, for when the maidens saw the beautiful bull, each felt within her a sudden desire to pet the creature. As they drew near their visitor, the maidens were enveloped by a fragrance that smelled sweeter than the flowers of the meadow.

Confident in his disguise, Zeus entered into the second phase of his carefully thought-out plan. He lapped Europa's hands and cheek. She smiled, stroked the white locks of his massive head, and gently kissed her new friend. Zeus could barely restrain himself.

Bowing low before his love, Zeus looked from her to his broad back, as if to suggest that she might sit there. Dare she mount the friendly creature? Europa could not decide. She turned to her companions and said, "Come, greet this gentle bull, which seems more a human than a beast. So gentle is he, so kind his eyes. He motions for me to mount him, and so I shall. Won't one of you join me, for surely it will be a most pleasant journey?"

Without hesitating another moment Europa jumped up and positioned herself on the enormous bull's back. Before she could stretch out a helping hand to one of the maidens who wished to join her, she felt herself being borne aloft. Zeus was not about to lose his prize! As soon as he felt the weight of his beloved Europa on his back, he leaped up and sped across the fields toward the water.

"Help me, *please*!" cried Europa. With one hand, she tightly clasped one of the bull's horns to steady herself; with the other, she desperately tried to reach the hands of her companions or anything that might help her escape.

Tears fell from her eyes as she realized all her efforts were in vain. "I must calm myself," she thought. "Perhaps he shall return me to my friends."

The young princess looked about her and braced herself for a sudden stop when she realized the coastline was only a short distance away. "Surely he will not enter the water!" she thought.

But Zeus never slowed his pace. Across the water he flew, his hoofs barely skimming the Mediterranean and Aegean seas. Europa sat motionless. Who was this bull for whom even the great seas calmed their waters? Barely a ripple could be seen anywhere. Then all of a sudden, the seas were astir with sea monsters, dolphins, and other creatures from the salty depths, all frolicking and dancing about the bull and his passenger. Zeus' disguise had not fooled them. They recognized his divine presence, as they had on many previous occasions, and rejoiced that he was once again in their midst.

The water nymphs also joined in the sport, riding the backs of all sorts of fanciful sea beasts. Even Poseidon, Zeus' brother and the god of the sea, left his home in the depths of the ocean to smooth the waves and clear a path for Europa and her divine companion. As always, the Tritons, the hoarse trumpeters of the deep, cavorted about Poseidon, playing bridal songs on their long conchs.

Europa could not join in the gaiety about her. She could barely move, think, or react. So far was she from any shore that she could see nothing but the deep blue water. Her clothes billowed out with the wind and acted like sails.

Finally, Europa summoned enough courage to ask her mount, "Where are you taking me? Who are you—a bull god? Surely you must be divine, for no earthly bull enjoys salt water or even dares venture into the smallest pond."

"Alas, fair maiden, I am Zeus. For love of you and to win your confidence, I took the disguise of a bull. Now let me take you to the Mediterranean island of Crete, where I myself was raised, and there win your heart." Europa did not resist.

As the bull and maiden soared above the waters to Crete, Europa remembered her dream. "I understand it now," she thought. "The woman who claimed she was my mother was so indeed. She was the continent Asia, where I was born. The other who affected me so deeply must have been this new continent where Zeus is taking me and to which I shall give my name."

Legend tells us that Europa remained on Crete for some time and there gave birth to three sons—Minos, the famed king of Crete; Rhadamanthys, one of the judges of the underworld; and Sarpedon, king of Lycia, a district in Asia Minor.

Legend also tells us that Europa's father ordered her mother and brothers to search the world for his lost daughter and not to return home to Phoenicia until they found her. Their journeys are the bases for several other Greek myths.

Eos Abandons Tithonos

ONE DAY EOS NOTICED THAT TITHONOS' HAIR WAS TURNING GRAY. SINCE IMMORTALS NEVER GREW OLD, THEY NEVER HAD GRAY HAIR. SUDDENLY SHE REALIZED THE DREADFUL TRUTH.

Early every morning, Dawn rises from her bed, dons her saffron-colored robe, and ascends her golden chariot pulled by two swift horses. As she speeds across the sky, her flowing veil disperses the night while her rosy fingers drop a gentle dew over the land. Fresh, cooling breezes follow her as she opens the gates of day, announcing to all the coming of the sun god in his chariot pulled by four horses.

In such a way did the early Greek poets describe their goddess of the dawn, whom they called Eos. The Romans, who also incorporated her tale into their legends, knew her as Aurora. This tradition of a dawn goddess who brought the first light of each day to both mortals and immortals has continued to be the subject of many literary works and paintings, especially those found decorating the ceilings of many of the grand palaces and stately homes of Europe.

The ancient authors frequently referred to the goddess of the dawn in their works. Most followed the example of the famed Greek poet Homer, who often had Eos introduce a new day in his epic poems, the Iliad *and the* Odyssey. *They also wrote of a tragic tale involving Eos.*

One morning as Eos sped across Troy, in Asia Minor, her pace slowed considerably when she caught sight of Tithonos, the son of Laomedon, the legendary king of Troy. Overwhelmed by a desire to meet him, she felt unable to continue her travels that day unless he joined her.

Tithonos readily accepted her invitation, then fell in love with her and asked her to marry him. Eos was overjoyed. However, Tithonos was a mortal, and she was an immortal. After carefully considering his proposal, she approached the king of the gods and begged him to make Tithonos immortal so that he could marry her. Zeus readily agreed.

One day, several years later, Eos noticed that Tithonos' hair was turning gray. Since immortals never grew old, they never had gray hair. Suddenly she realized the dreadful truth. She had asked for immortality, but she had forgotten to ask for perpetual youth. As the decades passed, Tithonos began to shrink and shrivel. So old did he become that his hands and feet became stiff.

Eos no longer wished to see her husband in this cruel state of existence, so she locked the unfortunate Tithonos in a room. Whoever passed the door heard his heart-rending pleas to Zeus, begging that the king of the gods allow him to die. Tradition says that Tithonos was finally changed into a grasshopper because his shrunken form so resembled that insect—thin, small, and noisy.

ENDYMION SLEEPS

1. Why was Endymion always sleeping when Artemis first saw him?
2. How did Zeus know that Artemis was not performing as she should?
3. What might be the reason the ancients included a tale of romance about Artemis in their mythology?
4. Why does Artemis continue to watch over Endymion's flocks?
5. Do you think Endymion made a wise choice in accepting Zeus' offer to have eternal youth and life as long as he remained asleep?

CUPID PIERCES HIS OWN HEART

1. Why did Cupid leave Psyche?
2. What tasks did Venus assign Psyche?
3. How did Psyche know her husband was the god of love?
4. The sequence of events in mythological stories does not always make sense. Facts and/or events sometimes contradict each other. Which two actions of Cupid seem contradictory?
5. Why do you think Cupid did not wish to reveal his identity to Psyche?

DAPHNE AND APOLLO

1. Why and how did Eros shoot Apollo?
2. Why did Daphne seek her father's help?
3. Was it necessary for Eros to shoot Daphne?
4. Why do you think the ancients chose to have Daphne become a tree and not a flower?
5. How do you think the myth of Daphne and Apollo developed? Why was it popular among the ancient Greeks and Romans?

IO AND ZEUS

1. How did Zeus hide himself and Io from Hera?
2. How did Io, after being transformed into a cow, make her identity known to her father?
3. Why did Hera believe Argos was the perfect guard for Io?
4. Hermes could have taken Io while Argos slept. Why does the myth of Io have Hermes kill Argos?
5. The ancients often used myths to explain natural phenomena. How do you think they interpreted the myth of Io and Argos?

THE ADVENTURE OF A BULL

1. Why did Zeus take Europa to Crete?
2. What did the two women in Europa's dream represent?
3. Why do you think Zeus tried to divert his attention from Europa?
4. What element does Zeus' ride across the waters add to the myth?
5. Why do you think Zeus chose the bull as his disguise?

QUESTIONS FOR DISCUSSION

1. Eros/Cupid was an important god in ancient mythology. Explain his role(s) in the stories in this chapter.
2. Every tale in this chapter includes a change of some sort. Identify and give the reason for each change.

SUGGESTED ACTIVITY

The ancients filled their world with mythological characters. Using the stories in this chapter, describe or draw a diagram of the Mediterranean world, placing the mythological characters in the appropriate locations (for example, Io in the Ionian Sea, Zeus as a bull carrying Europa across the Bosporus, Artemis carrying the moon across the skies).

FESTIVALS FOR THE GODS

Lupercalia

On the fifteenth day of the second month of the year, the ancient Romans celebrated the festival of Lupercalia, in honor of Lupercus. In Roman mythology, Lupercus was another name for Faunus, the god of the country, who protected shepherds and their flocks.

The Luperci were the religious men who presided over Lupercalia. Originally on this day, the god Lupercus was asked to help keep wolves away from the flocks. Lupercus (aptly named, as the Latin word for wolf is *lupus*) also was asked to provide a bountiful harvest and many lambs during the coming year. The sacred rites began at the Lupercal, a cave on the Palatine Hill, one of the seven hills of Rome.

Gradually, various traditions became associated with this festival. Goats were sacrificed. Strips cut from their skins were given to two youths born of noble parents. The Luperci then soaked a piece of wool in milk and wiped the boys' foreheads, which had been smeared with the blood of the sacrificed animals. The two boys, clothed in goatskin aprons, ran around the

Palatine Hill slapping anyone they met with their goatskin strips.

Why were goatskins used? Since goats are the most aggressive and toughest of the smaller animals tamed by man, the ancients felt that sacrificing them and using their skins as part of the religious ceremonies would be most effective in keeping wolves from their sheep. In time, it is said, the Romans began to believe that if these ceremonies could protect the flocks and help provide many lambs in spring, so might they help produce more Romans. Therefore, if these youths slapped or gently struck a woman with their goatskin strips as they ran around the Palatine Hill, she might give birth the next year.

The Roman name for the strips carried by the boys was *februa*, meaning "instruments of purification" (that is, objects that made what they touched pure and clean). The Latin verb to explain the action was *februare,* meaning "to purify." The Romans believed that these thongs had magic powers granted them by Iupiter's wife, Iuno, the queen of the gods. Since it was hoped that this festival would result in more births, Iuno was worshiped as the goddess of childbirth. In this role, she was called Februaria, from which we derive the name of the second month of the year.

HIGHLIGHT

Lupercalia and Valentine's Day

As the Roman Empire expanded, the Romans carried their customs to their conquered lands. Many of the people who inhabited these lands adopted or incorporated the Roman practices into their own culture. Many of Rome's provinces adopted the feast of Lupercalia. Because of its association with the hope of having more children, one can see how it gradually became associated with love and marriage. The people who lived during the Middle Ages believed that during the last two weeks of February, the birds began to mate. Perhaps it was also believed that at this time it was fitting for humans to seek husbands or wives.

Moreover, during this period, the priests of the early Christian Church wished to abolish all the festivals of the ancients. It was common practice to rename an ancient festival day and make it a special Christian day. To do this, the names of various saints were used. Since February 14 was already the day when some Christians prayed to a bishop of Rome named Valentinus, when it came to renaming the ancients' festival of Lupercalia, the choice of a new name was easy.

After the Roman emperor Claudius II had forbidden males of military age to marry (because it was believed married men preferred to remain at home rather than fight for Rome), Valentinus supposedly ignored the decree. According to legend, Valentinus secretly married all who came to him. As a result, he was condemned to death by the Roman emperor on February 14 in about A.D. 270.

No one knows the exact beginning of Valentine's Day, but by 1300, February 14 was regarded as a day of love. Love letters were written, and small gifts or mementos were sent. For many years, this day was taken very seriously, and many individuals waited and hoped for that special valentine to arrive.

Today Valentinus is rarely mentioned. But for weeks prior to February 14, red hearts and pictures of Cupid, the mischievous Roman god of love, abound, and we still hope to receive a valentine from that special someone.

Who Were the Salii?

FROM THE SKY FELL AN *ANCILE* (SHIELD). AS IT LANDED, A VOICE WAS HEARD SAYING THAT ROME WOULD BE SAFE AS LONG AS THIS SHIELD SENT BY MARS WAS PRESERVED.

In very ancient times, a terrible plague raged through Rome. Fearing that everyone would die, the Romans rushed to the temple of their protector, the god Mars. There they prayed and asked Mars for help. From the sky fell an *ancile* (shield). As it landed, a voice was heard saying that Rome would be safe as long as this shield sent by Mars was preserved. Not only did Mars send this shield, but that same day, March 1, he stopped the plague.

To prevent thieves from stealing this gift, the Romans commissioned a blacksmith named Mamurius Veturius to make eleven exact copies of the original shield. All twelve were placed in the temple of Mars in the Campus Martius at Rome, but only the special priests of Mars knew which was the original.

As a result of this incident, the Romans felt that all military expeditions should begin in the month of March. In fact, before a Roman general left on a military campaign, he touched the sacred shield with the point of his lance.

Twelve priests were assembled to guard the shield and to conduct the ceremonies held before an army left on a campaign. On March 1, these priests, dressed in embroidered tunics, bronze breastplates, and pointed helmets, led a procession through the center of Rome. Each priest had a sword at his waist and carried a staff in his right hand and a holy shield in his left.

The priests stopped at every altar and temple. In full armor, they did a war dance to expel all the evil spirits that might have entered the city during the winter. Since the Latin verb "to dance" is *salire*, these priests came to be known as the Salii. Not only did they dance, but they beat on their shields and sang special songs.

A few words have survived from these songs. Two lines from one song are:

Cume tonas, Leucesie, prae tet tremonti
Quom tibei dextumum tonaront

When you thunder, god of light, they tremble before you
When the lightning bolts come from your right hand

The procession continued through March 24, ending each day at an appointed place where the shields were kept in special houses until the next morning. At certain times during the three-week period, all horses, shields, spears, and other weapons used in battle were cleansed and made ready for new campaigns.

The word "religion" is derived from the ceremonies of the Salii. The Romans considered the days on which the twelve priests carried the shields solemn days called *dies religiosi* (religious days). Today we refer to these days as holidays—days of festivity, recreation, or religious ceremony when ordinary occupations are suspended.

The Eleusinian Mysteries

Death to those who revealed the secrets of Demeter's mysteries! The famed Greek military commander Alkibiades knew this well. Luck had him out of Athens when the verdict was given: death for having dared to imitate the secret rites of Demeter. As it was, only Alkibiades' property was confiscated. Others, however, were not so fortunate and were killed for their audacious crime.

According to tradition, Demeter sometimes punished the criminal herself. Several individuals who attempted to enter and see the forbidden rituals either died "accidentally" shortly thereafter or were afflicted by a fatal disease. If the punishment for revealing the mysteries had not been so severe, perhaps we would know more today. As it is, the details are sketchy.

In the beginning, Demeter's cult was local, but as her fame grew and the need for good harvests became more important, her worship spread to the surrounding countryside and other city-states. After Eleusis came under the dominion of Athens (about the seventh century B.C.), the Eleusinian mysteries became a Pan-Hellenic (all-Greek) institution. When Rome conquered Greece, the mysteries became a universal cult. For two thousand years, the mysteries of Demeter played a significant role in Greek history.

From all accounts, the rites were governed by strict, unchanging laws. Two families ministered and regulated the cult: the Eumolpids, descendants of Eumolpos of Eleusis, to whom Demeter herself revealed the mysteries; and the Kerykes, who traced their roots to Keryx. *Which* Keryx is the question. The Eleusinians said it was Eumolpos' younger son; the Athenians said it was the grandson of Athens' legendary King Kekrops. Other families also provided priests and priestesses, but they were of lesser rank.

The hierophant was the high priest. He had to be a member of the Eumolpid family, and he held the office for life. He alone had the right to show initiates the *hiera*, the revelation that completed the initiation. He alone could refuse to initiate anyone whom he considered unworthy.

As the cult grew, so did the number of priests and priestesses. The role of each varied according to his or her responsibilities. Some, such as the hierophant, were maintained at public expense, while others received fees from the initiates. Some could marry; others could not.

Initiation involved three stages: the Lesser Mysteries, the Greater Mysteries, and the highest mysteries, known as the *epopteia*. Little is known about the Lesser Mysteries. They were held once a year in Athens in the early spring (twice if there were a great many aspiring initiates), and their purpose was to cleanse, purify, and prepare the participants for the Greater Mys-

ACCOMPANYING EACH INITIATE WAS A SMALL PIG, WHICH ALSO WAS WASHED AND THEN SACRIFICED UPON ITS RETURN TO ATHENS.

teries, which were held in the early fall. Every fourth year, the Greater Mysteries were celebrated on a grand scale.

Prior to the Greater Mysteries, specially chosen messengers were sent to all Greek city-states (later they were sent throughout the Roman world) to announce the date of the celebration. A holy truce was proclaimed, allowing members and initiates to travel to and from the month-long celebration without being harmed. The messengers also asked each city-state for official delegations to be sent to Demeter and for tithes of the first fruits—all in thanksgiving for Demeter's help.

Only those guilty of homicide and those who did not speak Greek were barred from membership. Later this rule was extended to include foreigners. Membership was a personal choice; it was not hereditary. Group initiations were not allowed. Every *mystes* (initiate) had a sponsor, or *mystagogos*, who helped the initiate through the rites.

After Athens conquered Eleusis, the Greater Mysteries opened in Athens. The day before the celebration began, the hiera were carried in a procession in closed sacred cists (wicker containers) from Eleusis to Demeter's special sanctuary in Athens. Not much is known about the specific ceremonies held on the first four days, except that on the second day, each initiate and his or her mystagogos rode by carriage to the sea to wash in the purifying waters. Accompanying each was a small pig, which also was washed and then sacrificed upon its return to Athens.

On the fifth day, all walked the fourteen miles to Eleusis. The hiera traveled in a carriage. Singing, dancing, and other rituals took place along the way. It was an emotional time, and the anticipation was great. Only once, when Athens heard that Alexander the Great had destroyed the Greek city of Thebes, was the procession called off.

The sixth day was spent fasting, purifying, and sacrificing. Demeter's fast was recalled, along with her request for meal mixed with water and soft mint. It is believed that the initiates drank a concoction similar to Demeter's food. Wine was forbidden.

Then it was time for the initiation. We do not know the details of this rite, but it probably included a dramatic reenactment of Demeter's tale, perhaps accompanied by torches and sound effects. Then the hiera and other sacred objects were uncovered and revealed to the initiates.

Some of those present had been initiated the previous year but had spent the intervening months preparing for initiation into the highest degree of the mysteries, the epopteia. After the new initiates had viewed the sacred objects, they were asked to leave, while those who were returning for the epopteia remained. Again, we do not know the details of this event. The last day was spent praying and sacrificing for members who had died. On the ninth day, all returned home.

Members of the Eleusinian mysteries did not have to follow any prescribed rites or rituals, nor did they have to return to Eleusis. They lived as they had before, but their lives were enriched by their experience, and they were prepared, perhaps, to be better individuals and citizens.

Demeter of Eleusis

"Listen! I hear someone crying. There, over by the well. See, the old lady. Let's go and help her."

Quickly, the daughters of King Keleos ran to the well. "Come with us, dear lady. Lay aside your grief and join us at the palace. Our father rules this mighty and prosperous land, known to all as Eleusis." The old lady gratefully accepted the kind invitation but gave no reason for her tears.

"Mother, come and meet our new friend," the girls said.

Queen Metaneira was as kind and hospitable as her daughters. "Dear friend, lay aside your cares," she said. "Stay with us." Metaneira saw that her guest was no ordinary person. She recognized in her manner a godlike quality. "Yes, please stay and take care of our new baby son, Demophon."

The old lady readily consented. Her expression even changed. The sadness seemed to lift, if only a little.

At supper that evening, all was merriment and jesting. No one questioned the woman's refusal of wine or her request for a supper of meal and water mixed with soft mint.

The old lady seemed to love her new duties, and each day she looked happier. Metaneira, who had worried so about the woman's age affecting her infant son in some way, could hardly believe his phenomenal growth. Demophon was bigger, stronger, and healthier than any baby she had ever seen. What was the stranger's secret? No one knew, nor did anyone guess the truth.

Demeter (the old lady) was happy. She loved her new family, especially Demophon. Here, among caring mortals, she could forget the uncaring immortals, especially her brothers Zeus and Hades. Their scheme had been monstrous. Helios, the all-seeing god of the sun, had told her how Hades, the god of the underworld, had begged Zeus to help him steal the girl with whom he had fallen in love.

Tears came to Demeter's eyes as she thought of the girl, her beautiful daughter Persephone. Demeter had heard her desperate cries, but she was too late to save her. For nine days, she had searched everywhere, and then on the tenth day, Helios had revealed the dreadful truth.

"Good morning, friend," Metaneira whispered, for her friend looked deep in thought.

Demeter started and then remembered who and where she was. "Yes, it is a pleasant morning, Metaneira. Come sit with us."

"Friend, what is your secret?" Metaneira asked. "Demophon far surpasses all children his age and older."

"Metaneira, I do nothing other than what I would do for anyone I loved dearly," Demeter replied. But Metaneira was not convinced, and she vowed to discover the old woman's secret.

That night, she hid herself in her son's quarters and watched.

FAMINE SPREAD ACROSS THE LAND, FOR WITHOUT THE GODDESS OF THE HARVEST, THE EARTH COULD NOT PRODUCE. ZEUS REALIZED THAT HE HAD TO ACT OR LOSE THE HUMAN RACE.

Soon the old lady entered and fed Demophon supper. The odor of the food was different but very pleasant. Metaneira could not quite place it. The queen mother watched Demeter bathe Demophon, and then to her horror, she saw the old lady take Demophon and place him in the fire. Metaneira screamed and ran to her son's rescue.

"Untrusting, ungrateful mortal, you have just ruined your son!" Demeter cried. "Do you think that I, who love him dearly, could willfully harm him? No! I was making him a god. Since he has been in my care, I have fed him ambrosia, the food of the gods. Every night I have placed him in this sacred fire to burn out every trace of his human nature. I had almost succeeded, but your thoughtless actions stopped the process."

"Who are you?" asked Metaneira, trembling.

"I am Demeter, the goddess of the harvest. Go now and tell your husband, the king, and bid him build me a great temple."

King Keleos did so immediately, on the very spot Demeter had requested. The goddess entered the temple, turned, and locked the doors. She then made it known that she would remain within until she could see her daughter again.

Famine spread across the land, for without the goddess of the harvest, the earth could not produce. Zeus realized that he had to act or lose the human race. "Hades, we cannot allow the human race to die," he said. "You alone can help. Allow Persephone to visit her mother."

"But she has eaten of the pomegranate and so must remain here in the underworld," Hades replied.

"That is true," Zeus said, "but it need not be forever. Let her spend part of every year with her mother."

Persephone had been listening to this conversation but said nothing. Now she felt every nerve on edge as she waited for her husband's reply. "Yes, Zeus, that is fair. So be it!" Tears filled Persephone's eyes; she would see her mother again soon.

Inside the locked temple, Demeter thought she heard someone approaching. She looked from a window and saw Hermes, the messenger god, guiding Hades' golden chariot, and there beside him was her dear daughter.

Quickly, she ran to unlock the door. Out of the temple she flew, falling into the arms of her rejoicing daughter. "My dear Persephone, have you tasted any food in the underworld?" Demeter asked.

"Yes, mother, a few pomegranate seeds."

"Then you must return," Demeter replied. "But let us not think of that. Let us rejoice and enjoy our time together."

Before returning to Mount Olympos, Demeter walked about the fields of the earth and bade them produce abundant fruits and vegetables. The growing time would be short, for the earth was to become barren once Persephone returned to Hades, but there would be food to harvest.

To Demophon's brother, Triptolemos, Demeter entrusted her invention of the plow and the knowledge of agriculture. She also sent him a chariot pulled by fire-breathing winged dragons for him to roam the earth, teaching the secrets of sowing, reaping, and harvesting.

One day Demeter said to her

daughter, "Persephone, I must thank the people of Eleusis in a special way." Entering the palace, she said, "King Keleos, I owe you and your people my happiness. In gratitude, I entrust to you and your people the special secret rites and beliefs connected with my worship. Celebrate these mysteries in my honor and remember me."

And so it was that Eleusis became the center of Demeter's worship for two thousand years.

Why Spring?

Why are there great storms? Where does the sun go at night? Why are there four seasons for every year? These were very difficult problems for the ancients to solve. Even today, in various parts of the world where primitive societies still exist, these questions continue to be asked.

To understand the ancients' feelings, we must remember that they believed the world was flat. They had no computers or satellites and no meteorologists. They felt that everything they could not control was controlled by the gods and goddesses who lived on Mount Olympos.

When Zeus became angry, he hurled bolts of lightning. When the gods fought among themselves, the heavens resounded with thunder. When Apollo rode across the sky, his dazzling golden chariot was the sun spreading light across the land. To explain the four seasons, the ancient Greeks and Romans used the myth of Persephone.

Persephone had been captured by Hades, the god of the underworld. Every year, Hades allowed her to visit her mother, Demeter, on earth. When Persephone visited Demeter, she brought spring—radiant, beautiful, and alive. The grass turned green beneath her feet, the flowers bloomed in greeting, and blue skies overspread the world.

Then followed summer, with everything in full bloom. In autumn, after the crops were harvested, the farmers readied their fields for the cold of winter. Demeter bid her daughter farewell as winter, with its harshness, barrenness, and bleakness, descended upon the land.

In Rome, Demeter was called Ceres, from the Latin verb *creare*, "to create." Her daughter's name was Proserpina, the insurer of plentiful crops and a good harvest. Hades was called Dis by the Romans.

So that the Romans and Greeks might recognize each of the gods and goddesses easily, ancient artists and sculptors always placed certain items next to each deity. They pictured Demeter with poppies (the symbol of sleep and death) and with ears of corn (the symbol of fruitfulness). Persephone, if not with her mother, usually held a torch or a pomegranate (the symbol of death and rebirth).

Vesta and the Vestal Virgins

A VESTAL WAS NOT ALLOWED TO MARRY UNTIL SHE HAD COMPLETED HER THIRTY YEARS OF SERVICE AND HAD ELECTED TO ABANDON HER POSITION AS A VESTAL. FEW VESTALS EVER LEFT THE SERVICE OF VESTA.

One of the most important discoveries ever made was that of fire. Before the discovery of oil and electricity, fire was used to cook food, provide heat, and forge tools. Yet for centuries, primitive societies had great difficulty obtaining and maintaining a steady flame. Consequently, they believed that this great "civilizing element" was a divine gift from the gods.

To explain these thoughts, the ancients created and developed the myth about Prometheus, the fire-giving Titan. To ensure the continuity of this sacred flame, they established the worship of a goddess named Hestia in Greece and Vesta in Rome.

The ancients believed that this goddess, as the symbol of the special gift of fire, was best represented by the hearth (fireplace) and its fire. As a result, statues have been found of Hestia or Vesta.

In Rome, it was believed that Aeneas, the divine ancestor and founder of Rome, brought with him to Italy the fire necessary for his new community to survive. This fire, which came to represent the goddess Vesta, was preserved in a special temple. Whenever necessary, any villager could take some fire from the temple for household needs. If a villager's family was setting out for a new community, they always took with them some of this fire.

In later times, after the Romans became much more adept at building fires on their own hearths, the need for Vesta's fire was not so critical. However, out of respect, honor, and thanks to this goddess, the Romans continued to worship Vesta as the patroness and guardian of hearths and fires. A family's partaking of its daily meals around or near the hearth was considered a form of worship of Vesta.

Most temples were rectangular, but Vesta's were round, with an opening in the roof. Historians believe that this construction imitated the early Romans' round straw huts, which were built around a central hearth. The early settlers learned that a round room was more effectively heated and lighted than a rectangular room with its four corners. The Greek biographer Plutarch said that Vesta's temple was circular because it represented the universe and its central point—the element of fire, around which the planet Earth revolves.

The second king of Rome, Numa Pompilius, built Vesta's original temple in the center of Rome. Every June 9, the Vestalia was celebrated. During this festival, Roman matrons walked barefoot in a procession to Vesta's temple, where they prayed for her blessing on their households. Because wheat and bread were considered the mainstays of a community, millers and bakers especially observed her festival day. They crowned their mills and mules with garlands and loaves of baked bread.

To guard the eternal flame,

Numa decreed that young girls be chosen as priestesses of this goddess and her temple. Because Vesta was considered as chaste and pure as her fire and because the Romans believed that her brother Iupiter had decreed that she would never marry, it was considered essential that her attendants possess these same qualities.

Vesta's attendants were known as the Vestal Virgins. Each of the six priestesses was carefully selected. To be chosen as a candidate, a girl had to be between the ages of six and ten, have no physical defects, have been born of a free and respectable family, and have parents living in Italy. Each Vestal spent ten years learning the rules and practices that became her responsibility during the second ten years of service. Her last ten years were spent instructing the new Vestals. A Vestal was not allowed to marry until she had completed her thirty years of service and had elected to abandon her position as a Vestal. Few Vestals ever left the service of Vesta.

The Vestals dressed in long, flowing pure-white garments. Around their heads they wore bands from which ribbons hung. Their main task was to maintain, preserve, and honor Vesta's fire. Should the flame ever die out, the Vestal who had been guarding it was severely punished for her negligence. Every March 1, the old flame was allowed to die. A new fire was rekindled according to long-established rules. The Vestals used a combination of glass and the pure rays of the sun or created a flame from the friction caused by boring a hole in a piece of wood from a fruit tree.

Also entrusted to the Vestals' care were the original Penates, or household gods, which Aeneas had brought from Troy and whose safekeeping the Romans believed ensured the safety of the Roman state. Kept guarded in a special room in Vesta's temple that only Vestals were allowed to enter, these Penates were considered the symbolic guardians of the city's storeroom, where food and provisions were kept before being consumed by Vesta on her hearth.

The Palladium, a carved wooden image of the goddess Athena's friend Pallas, also was kept in this sacred room. Every Vestal was instructed to protect the Palladium with her life, for Rome's survival depended on its safety.

Every day, a sacrifice of plain, unadorned food was placed in a simple clay dish on the temple's hearth. The area around the hearth was cleaned daily with water poured from pitchers that the Vestals filled at fountains and streams, especially those sacred to Kalliope and her sisters, the Muses. When sacrificing, the Vestals covered their heads with woolen veils trimmed with a purple border.

Despite their rather strict and severe lifestyle, the Vestal Virgins were greatly honored by all Romans and granted many privileges. At the public games and in the theater, they had seats of honor. Anyone who attempted to harm them was sentenced to death. Although it was the Roman custom to bury the dead outside the city walls, these priestesses were allowed to be buried in the Forum, the religious and economic center of the city. Should a Vestal meet a criminal being led to his death, it was within her power to pardon the offender.

MANY FESTIVALS WERE HELD THROUGHOUT THE GREEK WORLD, BUT THE PANATHENAEA BECAME ONE OF THE MOST FAMOUS. IT DIFFERED FROM ALL OTHERS IN THAT IT WAS CELEBRATED ONLY IN ATHENS AND THE MAIN EVENT WAS A SOLEMN PROCESSION.

The Panathenaic Festival

Many centuries ago, at a time when gods mingled freely with humans, a boy was born to Hephaestos, the god of fire. Athena, the goddess of wisdom, had tried to prevent such an event. She had accepted Zeus' request never to marry and had ignored Hephaestos' declarations of love. But Hephaestos' desire to marry her was so great that through his desire alone, he produced an infant. How could Athena abandon such a child who had no true mother?

Aware of his parentage, yet hoping to prevent its disclosure, Athena gathered the baby in her arms, placed him in a basket, and entrusted the basket to the care of Pandrosos, one of the three daughters of Kekrops, the king of Athens. Athena gave Pandrosos the strict order never to open the basket.

Unfortunately, curiosity overwhelmed Pandrosos' two sisters, and one day they secretly entered the room where the basket was kept. Quickly, they lifted the lid. What a horrible sight met their eyes—a young babe encircled by a snake that instinctively lunged at the intruders. So shocked and terrified were they that they went mad, ran from the house, and leapt to their deaths from the Acropolis.

Athena then decided that she must rear the baby, who was named Erichthonios. Without further deliberation, she carried the young boy to a grove sacred to her. There she mothered and trained him until he had grown into a strong, intelligent man. Although she had not been able to make him immortal, she decreed that he would become a very prominent and powerful mortal and thus made him king of Athens.

In appreciation of Athena's loving care and concern, Erichthonios instituted the Panathenaea in her honor. Many festivals were held throughout the Greek world, but the Panthenaea became one of the most famous. It differed from all others in that it was celebrated only in Athens and the main event was a solemn procession. Sacrifices and gymnastic contests also were held. One of the most popular contests was the footrace known as the Lampadedromia. In relay-race fashion, the contestants were divided into teams, each of which was given a torch. The first team that reached the goal with the torch lit won.

Every four years, a more elaborate celebration was held. Called the Great Panathenaic Festival, it was held in Athens at the time of Athena's birthday, at the end of July or beginning of August.

Additional events were held at the Great Festival. Among these were equestrian contests, musical competitions, and even boat races. The winners of the musical contests received an olive crown set with gold. The victors in the athletic competitions were given a garland of olive leaves from the sacred olive trees of

Athena and a large, beautiful vase filled with olive oil. The figure of Athena was etched on the front of these vases. On the back of each was a representation of the contest for which it was awarded. Many of these Panathenaic vases are now housed in museums throughout the world.

The grand procession was held on the last day of the festival. The participants assembled near the entrance to the city of Athens. Among them were the victors in the games, the leaders of the sacrifices, the elders bearing olive branches, the young men carrying arms, and the young women known as Canephori balancing on their heads olive baskets that contained the sacred utensils, cakes, and other things needed for the sacrifices.

Husbands carried vessels containing offerings to Athena, and wives carried vessels of water for use in the ceremonies at the Acropolis. This solemn procession was immortalized in the sculptured marble frieze of the Parthenon.

For up to nine months prior to the festival, several young girls (sources differ as to the number) spent long hours in the house of Athena's priestess on the Acropolis weaving and embroidering a robe called a *peplos.* This was a long, shawl-like outer garment worn by Greek women. The magnificent designs on the peplos represented the deeds of Athena and Zeus and the great achievements of Athenian heroes. On the final day of the Panathenaea, the saffron-colored robe was brought down from the Acropolis and suspended, like a sail, from a ship that moved on wheels. Decorations had been placed in the area through which the procession would pass on its way to the Acropolis.

All moved slowly toward the Propylaea, the entrance to the Acropolis. There Athenians and non-Athenians separated, for only Athenians were allowed in this sacred area. Great sacrifices were held, and the peplos was presented to Athena and placed on her statue in the Parthenon. After all the ceremonies were completed, the participants attended a splendid banquet.

Saturnus and Saturnalia

Although the Romans borrowed very heavily from Greek mythology, they worshiped several gods before the arrival of the Greeks. Saturnus is considered to be an ancient Roman god. He was honored as the deity who taught the early Romans the art of agriculture, thereby introducing them to civilization. Saturnus established his first settlement on the Capitoline Hill. The inhabitants of this colony called the area Saturnia, a name frequently used by many ancient authors when they referred to Italy.

When Greek mythology began

to merge with Roman mythology, Saturnus came to be identified with the Greek deity Kronos. Legend tells how Saturnus fled to Italy after being defeated by Zeus. Ianus, a native Italian god and the god of beginnings, was believed to have welcomed Saturnus. Central Italy was supposedly named Latium because Saturnus first hid there after fleeing from Mount Olympus. (Latium is a derivative of the Latin verb *latere*, meaning "to hide.")

One day, so the tale goes, Saturnus disappeared. Legend says that the gods on Mount Olympus invited him to return. To honor Saturnus, the ancients constructed a great temple at the foot of the Capitoline Hill.

The Romans located their treasury under the temple because they believed that this kindly god would ensure their continued prosperity by preserving their wealth. Inside the temple was a statue of Saturnus. His hands held a crooked pruning knife, and his feet were wrapped in woolen ribbons. According to custom, most statues of Saturnus were hollow and filled with olive oil as a symbol of Italy's fertile soil.

The early Romans regarded Saturnus' rule as the Golden Age of Italy, and they decided to hold a great festival in his honor. They chose December because at that time farmers were able to relax after harvesting their crops.

THE EARLY ROMANS REGARDED SATURNUS' RULE AS THE GOLDEN AGE OF ITALY, AND THEY DECIDED TO HOLD A GREAT FESTIVAL IN HIS HONOR. THEY CHOSE DECEMBER BECAUSE AT THAT TIME FARMERS WERE ABLE TO RELAX AFTER HARVESTING THEIR CROPS.

Since early times, the festival of Sol Invictus (Sun Unconquered) had been held on December 25. Falling during the period of the winter solstice (the shortest day of the year), this holiday celebrated the fact that the sun god had once again overcome darkness and spring would return. It seemed appropriate that this great day would be preceded by rites in honor of Saturnus, the god of agriculture.

Saturnalia began on December 17. The Romans visited Saturnus' temple to worship his statue. Although by custom the Romans prayed with their heads covered to protect themselves and their thoughts from evil spirits, they worshiped the kind and generous Saturnus with uncovered heads. They even stripped the statue's feet of the woolen bands for this great festival. Once the religious services were completed, the remaining six days until December 24 were spent in merriment and feasting.

During Saturnalia, schools and courts were closed, business activities were suspended, and the Senate did not meet. No wars were started, and no criminals were executed. Slaves especially enjoyed Saturnalia, for they were considered free during this period. In some areas and homes, masters changed places with their slaves and served them dinner. These traditions recalled the Golden Age, when there were no social distinctions.

Everywhere one could hear cries and greetings of *"Io Saturnalia!"* Small candles were kept burning in the temples and in the homes of the wealthy. Gifts were exchanged. On street corners everywhere, merchants sold earthenware figures, clay dolls, and nuts for the Romans to give each other as Saturnalia presents, or *signillaria*, as they were called in Latin. Often a king was chosen to preside over the festivities in a home or larger area. Traditionally, this person was the one who, during the feasting, received the piece of cake with a bean or nut hidden inside.

LUPERCALIA

1. What were *februa*, and what was their purpose?

WHO WERE THE SALII?

1. Why did the Romans have twelve sacred shields?

THE ELEUSINIAN MYSTERIES/ DEMETER OF ELEUSIS/ WHY SPRING?

1. Who was eligible for initiation into the Eleusinian mysteries?
2. What were the three stages of initiation into the Eleusinian mysteries?
3. Why is so little known about the Eleusinian mysteries?
4. Why did the worship of Demeter attract many ancients to seek initiation in the Eleusinian mysteries?
5. Why was it necessary to establish a truce to coincide with the festivities accompanying the Eleusinian mysteries?
6. What terrible news did Helios bring Demeter?
7. What did Demeter plan to do with Demophon? Why?
8. How does the myth of Persephone explain the seasons of the year?
9. What does the myth of Demeter and Persephone tell you about the ancients' attitudes toward their gods?

VESTA AND THE VESTAL VIRGINS

1. How did Vesta's temple differ from other Roman temples? Why was it different?
2. Why did most Vestal Virgins choose to remain priestesses of Vesta after they completed their required years of service?

THE PANATHENAIC FESTIVAL

1. Why did Erichthonios feel indebted to Athena?
2. In ancient times, why were only Athenian citizens allowed to enter the Acropolis?

SATURNUS AND SATURNALIA

1. Why was Saturnalia celebrated in December?
2. How did the festivities of Saturnalia recall Italy's Golden Age?

QUESTIONS FOR DISCUSSION

1. How did many of the ancient festivals reflect the seasons—that is, the activities of the periods during which they were celebrated? Name at least two festivals that reflected the seasons and explain how they did so.
2. The ancients celebrated many festivals. Why do you think this was so? What purposes did the festivals serve?

SUGGESTED ACTIVITY

Celebrate one or more of the festivals discussed in this chapter in your classroom or with your family. Celebrate the festival on the same day it was celebrated in ancient times. Find other customs and/or rites associated with the festival(s) you chose.

TEACHER'S GUIDE

The myths included in ***The Myths and Legends of Mount Olympos*** focus on the lives and adventures of the principal gods and goddesses of the ancient Greeks and Romans. The first four chapters of the book are divided somewhat chronologically, beginning with Zeus' struggle for power and ending with tales involving his progeny. While it is not necessary to read the chapters in order, we recommend doing so. The tales involve so many of the same deities that it helps to associate a particular god or goddess with his or her parents and duties. The genealogy chart on page 6 and the map on page 9 are designed to serve as visual guides to help students see the relationships between the deities and to locate the areas mentioned in relation to today's world.

The theme emphasized in each of the first four chapters is listed below:

CHAPTER ONE: THE REIGN OF ZEUS
Zeus defeats the Titans and the Giants to become the ruler of the gods and goddesses on Mount Olympos and the humans he allowed to be created on earth.

CHAPTER TWO: CHILDREN OF THE OLYMPIANS
Zeus sires powerful gods and goddesses and assigns them a variety of tasks.

CHAPTER THREE: ADVENTURES OF THE GODS
The deities on Mount Olympos venture beyond their home, seeking adventure and interaction with others.

CHAPTER FOUR: ROMANCE AMONG THE GODS
Zeus and his offspring enjoy the company of mortals, with whom they occasionally fall in love.

The fifth chapter focuses on ancient holidays, describing their origins and the customs observed during each festival.

This book may be used in a number of ways: (1) as a separate unit to complement the study of Greek or Roman history and/or customs and beliefs being covered in the classroom; (2) as supplementary material assigned as extra reading inside or outside the classroom; (3) as a special day activity when students read or even re-create one or more of the myths in the classroom; (4) by month, as a class observance and reenactment of the festivals described in Chapter 5.

To complement the myths included in this book, have students read the English translations of the original sources of the myths. Such an activity will acquaint them with ancient authors and their works. Below is a brief list of sources to aid you in implementing this suggestion. Most libraries will have English translations of the ancient works men-

SOURCES

CHAPTER ONE

Creation Myth: Hesiod, *Theogony*, 108–506
Zeus versus Kronos: Hesiod, *Theogony*, 678–721
Zeus versus Giants and Typhon: Hesiod, *Theogony*, 820–880
Prometheus: Hesiod, *Theogony*, 507–616
Aeschylus, *Prometheus Bound* (a play)
Deukalion and Pyrrha: Ovid, *Metamorphoses*, I, 211–421

CHAPTER TWO

Hephaestos: Homer, *Iliad*, I, 571–611; XVIII, 369–379, 410–420
Hermes: *Homeric Hymn to Hermes*, number 4
Apollo: *Homeric Hymn to Apollo*, number 3
Artemis: *Homeric Hymn to Artemis*, number 27
Athena: *Homeric Hymn to Athena*, number 28
Dionysos: *Homeric Hymn to Dionysos*, number 7
Euripides, *Bacchae* (a play)

CHAPTER THREE

Arachne: Ovid, *Metamorphoses*, VI, 5–145
Hesperides: Apollodoros, *Library*, 5,11
Phaëthon: Ovid, *Metamorphoses*, I, 747–779; II, 1–366
Orion: Ovid, *Fasti*, V, 495ff.
Memnon: Ovid, *Metamorphoses*, XIII, 587–600

CHAPTER FOUR

Cupid and Psyche: Apuleius, *Metamorphoses* (also called *The Golden Ass*), number 4, 28–number 6, 24
Daphne and Apollo: Ovid, *Metamorphoses*, I, 452–567
Io and Zeus: Aeschylus, *Prometheus Bound*, 645–682, 848–851
Europa: Ovid, *Metamorphoses*, II, 843–875
Eos and Tithonos: *Homeric Hymn to Aphrodite*, number 5, 218–238

CHAPTER FIVE

Demeter and Persephone: *Homeric Hymn to Demeter*, number 2

tioned, especially of Ovid's *Metamorphoses* and the Greek plays. An excellent general reference, with the original sources listed, is *Classical Mythology*, 4th edition, by Mark P.O. Morford and Robert J. Lenardon (New York: Longman, 1991).

Each chapter contains a set of Resource Activities. For Chapters 1–4, a series of five questions complements each main myth. (In some instances, one set of questions refers to two myths that are closely related in subject matter.) The first two questions are easy, text-related questions, geared toward testing a student's retention of the basic facts mentioned in the myth. The third and fourth questions test the student's ability to retain and analyze what she or he has read. The fifth question allows the student to think more critically about the myth and give his or her opinion concerning the events and deeds described.

Following these are Questions for Discussion. Their purpose is to help the student see how the myths in the chapter interrelate, including the less important articles that do not have their own sets of questions. Students should be encouraged to think critically and to offer their own thoughts and beliefs.

Finally, at the end of every chapter is a Suggested Activity that should help relate the regular classroom curriculum to the myths in this book.

We changed the question format in Chapter 5 because the majority of articles are shorter and less detailed than those in Chapters 1–4. Two questions deal with the stories about Lupercalia and the Salii. A series of nine questions relate to the three stories involving the goddess Demeter. This is followed by a group of six questions referring to the remaining stories on major festivals. Within all these questions, you will find easy, text-related questions and thought/analysis questions.

The Answers section in this guide provides answers to all the questions accompanying each chapter. Students and teachers may, however, present additional information or elaborate on the answers given.

IMPORTANT NOTE ON SPELLING

The Greeks and Romans often had different names for each deity. We decided to use the Greek names in stories that take place in Greek-speaking areas and are attributed to Greek mythology and the Latin names in stories that take place in Latin-speaking areas and are attributed to Roman mythology. (Since most of these myths were well known in both Greek and Roman societies, the list on page 5 provides the Greek names and their Latin equivalents.) We also chose to follow the Greek spellings in the transliteration of Greek names into English. Hence, we have used *k* rather than *c* in names such as Herakles and Kekrops. We have kept the *os* endings in Greek names (for example, Olympos and Kronos) rather than using the later Latin adaptation *us*. (We have used the *us* endings only in the Roman myths.) The Latin alphabet does not include the letter *j*, so we have used *i* as the Romans did (for example, Iuno and Iupiter). For the names of mythological places, we have transliterated the Greek and Roman names according to the myth. For the names of real places, we have used the English spellings.

CHAPTER ONE
THE REIGN OF ZEUS

Before Zeus

1. Earth's name was Gaia; Heaven's was Uranos. The ancients thought of Earth as a disklike piece of land, circular and flat, and of Heaven as a dome of bronze or iron. Far beneath Earth lay the dark, unknown area of Tartaros.
2. The Giants were born from the blood that poured out of Kronos after he was fatally struck by his son Kronos.
3. Buried deep beneath life-giving Earth, Tartaros became the ancients' underworld, where all evildoers were sent. The darkness of the area and the unknown secrets added to the ancients' concept that evil alone could exist in such a place.
4. The ancients realized that life depended on the earth and the food it produced, the animals it nourished, and the streams it held. Therefore, it was only natural that in the beginning, they believed Earth had made the first land a good, habitable place.
5. The ancients believed that nature (the sky, the land, water) was controlled by supernatural powers. They reasoned that only enormous creatures with the ability and desire to terrify and destroy could produce storms, earthquakes, and the like. It followed that nature produced monsters to control a particular natural phenomenon.

Kronos Dethroned

1. Rhea tricked Kronos. Instead of the newborn Zeus wrapped in swaddling clothes, Rhea handed Kronos a stone wrapped in swaddling clothes.
2. The Kyklopes readied their anvils and fashioned thunderbolts for Zeus, a magic helmet for Hades, and a trident for Poseidon.
3. Atlas had led the Titans into battle for control of the world. As the defeated leader, Atlas supported the world for those who had won.
4. If Zeus had killed Kronos, perhaps another Titan would have taken command. Zeus realized he needed help. He was alone in the palace of Kronos and could have been overpowered by the other Titans. As cupbearer, he had the opportunity to upset Kronos' stomach and win back his siblings, who would aid him against the Titans.
5. Tartaros was deep and dark, but its population would certainly grow. Also, Hades' wealth was tremendous, as he had all the gold, copper, silver, diamonds, and other precious materials found beneath the earth's surface.

The Giants/Typhon

1. A plant. Gaia gave the Giants the fruit of a special plant that made them invincible. Its power faded only when a mortal fought them.
2. Zeus' daughter Athena was the only Olympian who did not fear the monster Typhon. But she knew she was not strong enough to defeat him. Therefore, she called her father a coward and berated him until she shamed him into challenging Typhon.
3. Gaia was the goddess of the earth. Therefore, she could nurture and produce whatever type of plant she wished. Since she could not control the other elements (sun, moon, rain) that contributed to a plant's growth, her powers were somewhat limited.
4. Perhaps. Without the use of his legs, Zeus could not move. He could not rally his Olympians. He could not lead them into battle. Typhon did not have to worry much about confining Zeus, as his options for escape were minimal.
5. Gaia, the name of the goddess representing the earth, was the mother of all the Giants. Therefore, the ancients reasoned that the land that gave birth to each Giant produced a special bond that was immortal. Only when that bond was severed was he vulnerable and mortal.

The Gifts of Prometheus and Epimetheus

1. Prometheus stole fire from Hephaestos, the god of fire, because he wanted his creation, the human race, to have something that would allow it to develop and improve the world.
2. Zeus asked Hephaestos to create a woman out of clay. He then asked each Olympian to endow her with a special gift.
3. Yes. Prometheus wanted humans to be allowed to keep the tasty, nourishing meat of the ox. He wanted his creation, the human race, to survive. The Olympians did not need meat or even bones to survive, but humans did. Prometheus only wanted to satisfy the jealous Olympians.
4. According to the ancients, Zeus and the

Olympians jealously guarded their power. They saw creatures that walked on two legs (as they did) and knew the secret of keeping a fire going as a threat to their supremacy. But if these creatures believed that they had to sacrifice to the Olympians, they would consider themselves dependent on the Olympians and not as powerful.

5. The ancients could not explain or understand many of nature's forces, which produced many hardships—disease, crop failures, constant warfare. Yet they always hoped conditions would improve. The story of Pandora's box is thought to have been created to explain the human emotion of hope, an emotion that is almost impossible to kill or stifle.

Deukalion and Pyrrha

1. Zeus feared for Mount Olympos. If he used his thunderbolts, the fire they would cause might burn out of control and reach the heavens. An outpouring of water could be confined to the land.
2. Deukalion's father was Prometheus, the Titan whom many ancients credited with creating the human race. Since Prometheus did not want all of his creations to be destroyed, he told his son of Zeus' plan to flood the world and counseled him to build an ark.
3. Whether Zeus, the Olympians, or Prometheus created humans, the ancients felt that Zeus valued life as a gift that should be respected and held sacred. He did not believe humans should involve themselves in fraudulent and evil actions against each other. Since the people who lived during the Iron Age were doing just that, Zeus resolved to rid the earth of these people and create a race that valued life more highly.
4. The ancients felt that by covering their heads, evil spirits and other distractions could not interfere in their sacrificial rites.
5. For the ancients, this would have been an appropriate resting place. Delphi was sacred to Apollo. As the god of the sun, Apollo was the god most needed to make the earth productive again. Apollo also was the god of prophecy and knew the future of everything, including the human race. Themis, as the early patroness of Delphi and the goddess of justice, was the appropriate goddess to receive the just Deukalion's first prayers.

QUESTIONS FOR DISCUSSION

1. According to the ancients, Gaia made the earth productive by using her goodness and creating love. Gaia produced the Titans, the Hekatoncheires, and the Kyklopes. Gaia aided in the downfall of Uranos and Kronos, both of whom disliked competition or new life. Gaia also mourned the death of every creature and sought to avenge wrongs. From the earth, Prometheus created humans, and from stones and earth, Deukalion and Pyrrha repopulated the world.
2. Answer should include these elements: (a) Prometheus' counseling of Zeus against the Titans, which contributed to Zeus' victory; as a result, Zeus commissioned him to create humans; (b) Prometheus' decision to make humans walk on two legs; (c) Prometheus' stealing of fire twice; (d) Prometheus' counseling of Deukalion to build an ark to survive the flood.

CHAPTER TWO

CHILDREN OF THE OLYMPIANS

Hephaestos: The God of Fire

1. As Zeus' wife, Hera was the queen of the Olympians. She was also the patroness of marriage and protected and aided women who sought her advice.
2. He fashioned a golden chair with invisible chains. When his mother sat in the chair, the chains wound around her body. Only Hephaestos knew the secret of unlocking the chains.
3. Ares, as god of war, was portrayed as acting brusquely and harshly. He did not feel any empathy for others. Hephaestos was not a cruel god, but he had been wronged. His chains did not hurt Hera, and he wished to teach her a lesson. Dionysos was a jovial god. Life was a party for him. His good nature so calmed Hephaestos that the latter even drank his wine. Then he was able to convince Hephaestos to free Hera.
4. The Olympians were much like humans in their actions and feelings. In addition, they could be quite cruel. For example, Hera disowned her son because he was lame; Zeus was so angered by Hephaestos' siding with Hera against him that he threw Hephaestos from Olympos; Dionysos disregarded the feelings of both sides; Hephaestos meant

his chair to confine Hera indefinitely as fitting revenge for her treatment of him.

5. The ancients attempted to explain natural phenomena by attributing them to actions of the gods. By having Hephaestos have workshops in various locations around the Mediterranean world, they could say that volcanic activity and other fiery occurrences resulted from Hephaestos' work at his forge.

The Inventive Hermes

1. Hermes climbed out of his cradle and offered Apollo the lyre he had made. He also promised to return the cattle.
2. Snakes represent rebirth, for snakes shed their old skins for new ones. Doctors try to make the bodies of ill people whole or "new" again. The wand of the caduceus represents Apollo's gift of a magic wand to Mercury and symbolizes the magic needed to make an old body new. Doctors felt that the wand and the snakes symbolized their profession.
3. The ancients honored Hermes as the messenger god. To illustrate that Hermes was fleet of foot, the tale told of his hopping out of his cradle, running across a field, creating something extraordinary, getting food that was more substantial than "cradle food," and then rushing back to his cradle. All these acts portray an agile, quick-witted god.
4. As the messenger god, Hermes saw everything on Mount Olympos and around the Mediterranean world. His role as a guide added to his knowledge of what was going on. Also, the ancients portrayed him as impartial, so both sides in any situation often sought his aid. His interaction with humans as a messenger, as guide to the underworld, and as patron of merchants, among other things, led to his being considered reliable and trustworthy.
5. As the messenger god, Hermes traveled all thoroughfares. His early escapades with the lyre and the cattle proved his sharp mind and cunning ways. Since successful thieves need to possess these characteristics, they chose Hermes as their patron.

The God Apollo/Artemis: The Goddess of the Hunt

1. Hera forbade any land to allow Leto to settle there, caused workers to muddy Leto's drinking water, and sent a serpent to pursue her.
2. The ancients worshiped Artemis as the goddess of the hunt and the moon and the patroness of young people. They also called on her to help at childbirth.
3. Apollo was the god of prophecy. He had many worshipers, and he could not attend to their needs or requests personally. He needed intermediaries—people who could listen to the worshipers and counsel and advise them. Apollo used his priests as the bearers of his prophecies. They would act as the messengers of his tidings to the human race.
4. Apollo, as the sun god, ruled the heavens during the day; Artemis, as the moon goddess, ruled the heavens at night. Apollo was the patron of hunters; Artemis was the goddess of the hunt. Apollo was the god of light and civilization; Artemis protected youths—those who would fashion and mold the future.
5. Apollo and Artemis were two of the chief gods on Mount Olympos. Their father was Zeus. To show their importance and to demonstrate how the gods worked together and complemented each other, the ancients created various episodes involving other gods and goddesses. Humans were included to illustrate the part humans played in the affairs of the Olympians. Such interaction made human worshipers feel closer to the gods and helped them identify with them.

Athena: The Goddess of Athens

1. Gaia warned Zeus that if he and Metis had a second child, it would be a boy who would eventually dethrone Zeus. Zeus promptly swallowed Metis, who was pregnant with Athena.
2. Athena gave Athens the olive tree. Athens and Greece were known for their olive oil. Economically, Athena's gift helped Athens prosper far more than Poseidon's spring of salt water.
3. Hephaestos, a master craftsman, was able to fashion all types of materials to perfection. Hermes knew that great skill and accuracy were required to operate on Zeus' head, which is probably why he chose Hephaestos to perform the task.
4. Wars were common in ancient times, as was the struggle for power. The Greeks believed that Athena was born prepared to defend her people. But war must be tempered by wisdom. Therefore, the Greeks worshiped Athena as the goddess of wisdom, for she had sprung right from Zeus'

head. As the goddess of war and wisdom, Athena counseled forethought and moderation in battle and in victory.

5. Athena was the patroness of Athens. It was only fitting that she embody the attributes of the city-state. The statue was tall and majestic, symbolizing the Athenians' image of their city-state. The statue of the goddess Nike in her left hand symbolized an Athens victorious over its enemies. The lance in her right hand showed that Athena and the Athenians were prepared to fight to preserve their freedom. The aegis showed that just as Athena was immortal and indestructible, so too was Athens.

Dionysos' Birth/Dionysos and His Followers

1. Semele was a mortal. The clothes Zeus wore among the Olympians were so dazzlingly bright, the thunderbolts so fiery, and the lightning bolts so hot that Zeus knew Semele's mortal body could not withstand them. He knew her request meant death.
2. Pirates roamed the Mediterranean Sea, capturing and seizing ships, especially merchant ships, for their cargo. Frequently, the pirates also took captives, especially when they thought they could ransom a captive for a considerable sum. The pirates' pilot sensed something different about Dionysos' demeanor and asked Dionysos' pardon.
3. Semele did not trust Zeus' word. When her "nurse" (Hera in disguise) cast doubts on Zeus' identity, Semele fell victim to these doubts. Even when Zeus begged her not to force him to comply with her request, Semele was adamant that he do so. The doubt Hera had created caused Semele to cast reason aside.
4. The pirates kidnapped Dionysos. Since Dionysos was the god of wine and vegetation, he decided to punish the pirates using what was most dear to him. Therefore, he had the vines and tendrils of his luscious grape vines entangle the rigging and workings of the pirates' ship.
5. As the god of wine, Dionysos was considered the patron of those who enjoyed drinking. Festivals celebrated in honor of Dionysos usually involved drinking. This led to boisterous behavior that was more erratic and wilder than normal behavior.

QUESTIONS FOR DISCUSSION

1. a) Zeus disguised himself as a cuckoo bird to woo Hera.

   b) Hermes used a turtle and an ox hide to fashion his first lyre.

   c) Hermes stole some of Apollo's cattle.

   d) Hermes separated two snakes with his wand and used it as his symbol.

   e) Zeus changed farmers who were cruel to Leto into frogs.

   f) Hera sent a serpent to harass Leto.

   g) Dionysos changed himself into a lion and caused a bear to appear on board the pirate ship. As each pirate dove into the sea to escape the lion and the bear, he was changed into a dolphin.

   h) Apollo slew a serpent monster near Mount Parnassos.

   i) Apollo changed into a dolphin to recruit priests for his temple at Delphi.

   j) Artemis' altars were heaped with hunters' prizes from the animals they killed.

   k) The Muses' companion was Pegasos, the winged horse.

   l) King Pieros' daughters were changed into magpies after they lost a singing contest to the Muses.
2. a) Hera, a goddess, and Zeus, a god, were the rulers of gods and men.

   b) Iris, a goddess, and Hermes, a god, both acted as messengers for the gods.

   c) Artemis, a goddess, and Apollo, a god, were the patrons of hunting.

   d) Athena, a goddess, and Ares, a god, were the patrons of war.

CHAPTER THREE

ADVENTURES OF THE GODS

The Master Spinner

1. Idmon's specialty was purple dye. This dye was scarce, and therefore expensive, so not all dyers could afford to use it. In addition, in very ancient times, only kings and nobles wore purple. To be the dyer of the king's clothes ensured one's reputation.
2. Athena calmly approached Arachne disguised as an old woman and offered her advice. Arachne answered her haughtily and openly mocked Athena, boasting that she could weave better than the goddess.

Even when Athena made herself known, Arachne, after recovering from the initial shock, held to her boast.

3. Athena wanted to give Arachne a chance to repent. By assuming a mortal shape, Athena could pretend that she was an admirer who wished to offer advice. Old women commonly gave advice in ancient times, and the advice of an old nursemaid was considered especially sound and worthwhile.
4. Athena aimed to punish Arachne for presuming that she, a mortal, could outperform Athena, an immortal. Therefore, in all her scenes, immortals won and mortals lost. Furthermore, the central motif depicted her as being especially powerful by defeating another immortal, Poseidon. Arachne chose purple as her basic color—the color reserved for mortal kings and nobles and immortal gods. Arachne used tales of the gods' misdeeds as her theme, for she thought that Athena's attitude was wrong.
5. Students will have various answers to this question. Remind them, however, that as a spider, Arachne will die, but her legacy as a master spinner will survive in her spider descendants.

Maidens of the West

1. The great goddess Earth gave Hera the tree as a wedding present. As this tree had leaves of gold and produced golden apples, Hera was afraid that someone might steal her fruit or, even worse, destroy her tree. Therefore, she wanted guardians around the tree all the time.
2. When Atlas returned to Herakles with the golden apples, he did not intend to take the world back. Herakles tricked Atlas by asking him to hold the world for a minute so that he (Herakles) could adjust the pad on his shoulder. Without thinking, Atlas agreed, and Herakles quickly left.
3. The ancients depicted Rumor as invisible, with a thousand eyes and tongues. Rumors are invisible, for no one can actually see a tale told from person to person, especially as it grows. In addition, people everywhere spread rumors. To see and tell all that went on, the goddess had to have many eyes and tongues.
4. Atlas took his responsibility of supporting the world very seriously. He carefully explained to Herakles how to kneel and move so as not to disrupt the world order. When Atlas' daughters pleaded with him not to return to Herakles, he conscientiously explained that he was obliged to give Herakles the apples. After Atlas was tricked by Herakles, he reassumed his burden without any show of anger that would disrupt the world.
5. Herakles was a mortal, but in this myth, he interacts with immortals. The purpose of the ancients was to make Herakles a larger-than-life hero. Herakles dutifully obeys the oracle and performs incredible tasks without complaining. We see his clever mind as he figures out just whom to ask for advice, how best to approach the Hesperides, and what means to use to deceive Atlas. He is not deterred from his purpose, as he imprisons Nereus until he divulges the location of Hera's tree.

Phaëthon's Ride

1. Phaëthon's friend Epaphos, the son of Zeus and Io, taunted him by calling him a liar. Everyone knew that Zeus was Epaphos' father, but Phaëthon had no proof that he was Helios' son. Phaëthon tried to prove his identity by getting Helios to allow him to drive the sun chariot.
2. Earth (Gaia) begged Zeus to save her from being scorched by the heat from the sun chariot. Realizing that Earth would be destroyed if he did not act, Zeus hurled his thunderbolt at Phaëthon.
3. Helios welcomed Phaëthon warmly after learning of the taunting he had received. Helios seemed to want to make up for his neglect by offering to grant whatever Phaëthon asked. Helios tried to dissuade his son from driving the chariot, but eventually he relented.
4. The damage done by Helios' ride accounted for many physical phenomena that were otherwise unexplainable. The areas scorched by the sun chariot became deserts; waterways bore down into the earth and later provided springs for the ancients; the skin of the earth's inhabitants who were burned turned black.
5. In ancient times, the sun rising mysteriously in the east and then setting hours later in the west stirred people's imagination. Since horses and chariots were very familiar to them, and since they had a tendency to explain natural phenomena as acts of supernatural beings, the idea developed that a particular deity must ride across the sky

every day with the sun. But carrying the sun would be difficult, so the sun became a fiery chariot carrying the deity. When the god steered the chariot too close to the earth, the weather was hot. When he steered the chariot too far from the earth, it was cold.

The Mighty Orion

1. Hyrieus was a widower who had vowed never to marry again. His one wish was to have a son. His guests (Zeus, Poseidon, and Hermes) took the hide of the ox Hyrieus killed and ordered him to bury it, then return to the site in ten months. When Hyrieus returned, a boy was pushing his way up through the earth.
2. Orion begged the gods who had created him to help cure his blindness. The gods did not restore his sight but advised him to seek the sun and its rays.
3. According to the ancients, Artemis was the goddess of the hunt and cared little about love, marriage, or men. Her adherents followed her example and did not worship Aphrodite, the goddess of love. Because Merope's father refused to allow Orion to marry his daughter, Orion decided he should become a devotee of Artemis. In addition, as moon goddess, Artemis was partial to darkness, and Orion had lived in darkness while he was blind.
4. With Orion as a constellation, Artemis, as goddess of the moon, could watch over Orion and see him every night. Also, as a constellation, Orion achieved immortality as a heavenly body.
5. The ancients thought that the gods did this so that they could experience how mortals treated one another. From mortals' treatment of each other, especially strangers, the gods could judge them. The gods rewarded those who were honest, generous, and kind and punished those who were stingy and mean.

Dawn's Tragic Loss

1. Hephaestos, the god of fire, made Memnon's armor. Hephaestos was the best craftsman among the gods and made all their armor. As Memnon was the son of a goddess, he too received Hephaestos' gift of armor. (N.B. Hephaestos also fashioned Achilles' armor, as Achilles' mother was the goddess Thetis.)
2. Zeus commanded Memnon's ashes to whirl up into the air, where they were changed into birds that split into two groups. These groups fought each other until they fell back to earth as offerings to Memnon's ashes. Every year, according to the ancients, birds known as the Memnonides returned and performed the same ritual.
3. In ancient times, it was customary for one soldier on one side to battle another soldier on the opposing side. Both armies sat on the field and watched this battle. Often the battle began when a soldier on one side (the hero) challenged one of the enemy's soldiers.
4. Eos was the goddess of the dawn, a very brief part of the day that many people do not even notice. Perhaps she felt that night and day would still exist even if she did not clear the night's shadows or open the way for the sun. Her powers were few in comparison with those of the mighty Olympians.
5. The ancients' had not advanced enough scientifically to explain all the natural occurrences in the world. Therefore, they created myths to explain these occurrences. The dewdrops that appeared in the morning resembled tears. Because they were seen only at and immediately after dawn, the ancients said they were Eos' tears.

QUESTIONS FOR DISCUSSION

1. a) Arachne became a spider. Weavers, designers, and craftspeople have used spider-web patterns as inspiration for their creations for centuries.

   b) Phaëthon's sisters, the Heliades, became poplar trees. Their salty tears hardened and turned to amber. Amber is the hardened resin of ancient pine trees and is prized today for making jewelry and ornaments. Amber that contains fossilized insects is especially valuable.

   c) Orion became a constellation. The constellation's position at daybreak in the eastern sky denotes summer's beginning. When the constellation rises at midnight, it is a signal that fall has arrived and it is time for harvesting grapes and making wine. When the constellation rises late at night, it is winter and the time of storms.

   d) Eos, the goddess of the dawn, was unable to control her mourning for Memnon. Dewdrops provide a small amount of moisture and may even contribute to rock erosion in dry, rocky areas.

e) The Pleiades became a constellation. The position of the constellation continues to guide farmers and sailors. Its rising in the middle of May signals the beginning of the sailing season and the time to sow crops. Its setting at the end of October signals the end of sailing and the approach of harvest time.

2. a) Maidens of the West: Hera received the special tree as a gift when she married Zeus. Eurystheus, who told Herakles to snatch the golden apples, was the great-grandson of Zeus. Atlas had been condemned by Zeus to hold the world on his shoulders. Herakles was the son of Zeus.

   b) Phaëthon's Ride: Epaphos, who taunted Phaëthon, was Zeus' son. Zeus hurled his thunderbolt to stop Phaëthon and the sun chariot. Zeus commanded Helios to continue leading the sun chariot after Phaëthon's death. Zeus repaired the damage caused by Phaëthon's ride.

   c) The Mighty Orion: Zeus was one of the disguised guests of Hyrieus. Zeus, Poseidon, and Hermes promised to grant Hyrieus' wish for a son.

   d) Dawn's Tragic Loss: Zeus weighed the fate of Memnon and Achilles during their battle at Troy. Zeus answered Eos' plea and changed Memnon's ashes to birds.

   e) The Pleiades: Zeus answered the Pleiades' plea to help them flee from Orion by changing them into doves.

CHAPTER FOUR

ROMANCE AMONG THE GODS

Endymion Sleeps

1. Endymion was a shepherd. Since Artemis was the goddess of the moon, she traveled across the sky at night, the time when Endymion would be sleeping in the fields with his sheep.
2. When Zeus noticed that the arrival of moonlight in some areas was later than usual, he began to wonder what Artemis was doing. When he saw that her complexion, usually ruddy from the hunts of the day, was pale, he knew something was wrong.
3. The ancient Greeks and Romans tended to personalize their gods. They attributed human characteristics to them. Artemis was always worshiped as the goddess of the hunt and as one who did not think of love. Giving her a love interest made her more human—perhaps more approachable by her worshipers.
4. According to mythology, when Endymion chose eternal life, he remained a shepherd. Since he would never awake, his flocks needed care and protection, especially to ward off animals of prey. Artemis also cared for the newborn lambs.
5. No correct answer; each student will have his or her own opinion.

Cupid Pierces His Own Heart

1. Cupid had Psyche promise never to try to discover his identity. Psyche listened to her sisters and secretly sneaked a look at the sleeping Cupid. Inadvertently, she dropped oil on his shoulder as she did so and woke him. Realizing Psyche had broken her promise and accusing her of not being trustworthy, Cupid left. Cupid felt that love could not exist under these conditions.
2. Venus assigned Psyche these tasks: (a) to sort an enormous pile of seeds; (b) to fetch three tufts of golden wool from certain sheep; (c) to fill a bottle with water from the Styx; (d) to ask Proserpina to fill a box with her beauty.
3. The ancient Greeks and Romans knew their mythology. Psyche was naturally credited as knowing it, too. When she saw the arrow (and presumably the bow) at the foot of the bed, when she saw how handsome her "husband" was when he awoke and spread his golden wings, and when he flew away, she knew he must be Cupid, the god of love.
4. When Psyche dropped the oil on Cupid, he awoke and flew off. But while Venus was assigning Psyche the tasks, Cupid was confined to a room and did not have the strength to use his wings. How was he able to fly back to Olympus the first time?
5. Cupid loved Psyche and did not wish to lose her. She was mortal, and he was immortal. Cupid knew that he could not marry her officially on Mount Olympus. He also knew that his mother, Venus, would never allow such a marriage. If Psyche knew his true identity, she might tell someone about their relationship. Venus would find out, and Cupid might never see or be with Psyche again.

Daphne and Apollo

1. Apollo ridiculed Eros when he saw Eros stringing his bow. Eros resolved to punish Apollo. He shot Apollo with a sharp golden arrow to make him fall in love with Daphne. Eros shot Daphne with a blunt, lead-tipped arrow to make her not fall in love with Apollo.
2. Daphne had vowed to remain single. She had no intention of returning Apollo's love. Therefore, when Apollo gave chase and came closer and closer to her, she realized she needed help. Her only chance of escape was to be turned into another form, and she trusted her father to do this. He heard her pleas and changed her into a laurel tree.
3. Yes. Although Daphne had already vowed to remain single and to be a follower of Artemis, perhaps Eros shot his arrow to make sure that she did not change her mind and that Apollo's pleas would go unanswered.
4. A tree is tall and majestic and can be thought to contain a personality within its bark. A tree can live far longer than a flower and can be seen from a distance. If tall, full, and green, it can "reign" over everything around it. These may be some of the reasons why Daphne became a laurel tree.
5. The laurel tree was an important part of the ancients' religious and political life. Winning athletes were crowned with its leaves. Victorious political and military leaders also received laurel crowns. As a tree, its leaves are always green and shiny. The myth of Daphne and Apollo definitely helped to explain this difference from other trees and to heighten the laurel's importance among people.

Io and Zeus

1. Zeus had a thick cloud cover the area where he and Io met. The cloud did not move, however, and this aroused Hera's curiosity.
2. Io used her front foot to scratch her name in the sand.
3. Argos had one hundred eyes. When he slept, only two eyes closed at a time. Therefore, no one and nothing could approach the cow unnoticed.
4. In mythology, the peacock is Hera's favorite bird. The ancients used Argos' eyes to explain the "eye" at the end of each peacock tail feather. If Hermes had not killed Argos, that explanation would not have been possible.
5. The wanderings of Io in her cow form mirrored those of the moon, for the ancients often represented the crescent of the new moon as a cow's head with horns. The eyes of Argos were the stars, forever twinkling and standing guard over Io.

The Adventure of a Bull

1. Zeus' mother, Rhea, had hidden Zeus on the island of Crete so that his father, Kronos, would not find and destroy him. (Kronos had been told that one of his children would dethrone him.) Zeus felt close to Crete and wanted to share it with Europa.
2. The first woman who said she was Europa's mother represented Asia, the continent where Europa was born. The other woman who said that Zeus wanted Europa to follow her represented Europe, the continent where Zeus carried Europa and to which she gave her name.
3. Zeus knew how jealous Hera was and how she hurt or punished anyone she discovered with him. Perhaps Zeus did not want to expose Europa to such treatment.
4. The ride was full of pageantry. All the creatures and gods of the deep rose above the waters to pay homage to Zeus, whom they recognized even though he was disguised as a bull. The pageantry emphasized Zeus' love for Europa and foreshadowed the importance of their relationship and their future offspring.
5. The bull is strong, powerful, and dominant—all characteristics of Zeus himself. Bulls also were associated with Crete—for example, the Minotaur at Knossos on Crete and the famed Cretan bull dancers.

QUESTIONS FOR DISCUSSION

1. a) Artemis fell in love with Endymion.
   b) Cupid fell in love with Psyche and vice versa.
   c) Apollo fell in love with Daphne.
   d) Zeus fell in love with Io.
   e) Zeus fell in love with Europa.
   f) Eos fell in love with Tithonos.
2. a) Endymion changed to a creature (human in form) that would survive forever, although he would never awake. This change was to please Artemis.
   b) Psyche was given ambrosia and nectar, which changed her from mortal to immortal, so that she could marry Cupid.
   c) Daphne was changed into a laurel tree to escape Apollo.

d) Io was changed into a cow to escape detection by Hera. Argos' eyes became the "eyes" at the end of the tail feathers of the peacock. Hera did this to immortalize him.

e) Zeus changed into a bull so that he could whisk Europa away and woo her.

f) Tithonos, who had eternal life but not eternal youth, became a grasshopper (tradition says Zeus did this) after shriveling up with old age.

CHAPTER FIVE

FESTIVALS FOR THE GODS

Lupercalia

1. *Februa* were strips of goatskin used during the ancient Roman festival of Lupercalia. Two boys, dressed in goatskin aprons, ran around the Palatine Hill in Rome hitting whomever they met with these strips.

Who Were the Salii?

1. According to the Romans, an *ancile* fell from the sky in ancient times. A voice spoke out, saying that Mars had sent the shield and that Rome would be safe as long as the shield was protected. Because the Romans wanted to prevent it from being stolen, they had eleven exact copies made. Since only the priests of Mars knew which was the original, all were held sacred.

The Eleusinian Mysteries/Demeter of Eleusis/Why Spring?

1. At first, everyone except criminals guilty of homicide and people who did not speak Greek were eligible for the Eleusinian mysteries. Later, membership was extended to include foreigners. Membership was by choice, not hereditary. "Foreigner" was originally a very broad term. At first, everyone except Eleusinians were foreigners. Gradually, the term came to mean those who did not speak Greek and then, when Greece was subject to Rome, anyone who was not a Roman citizen.
2. The three stages of initiation were as follows: (a) the Lesser Mysteries (held every spring, twice if there were many initiates); (b) the Greater Mysteries (held in the fall for nine days, on a grand scale every fourth year); and (c) the *epopteia* (secret rites; we do not know the details of these, but during the process, the highest rank of initiates viewed the sacred objects).
3. Initiates and members were forbidden to reveal any of the rituals involved. Death was the penalty for anyone who did so. The law also forbade anyone to imitate the secret rites.
4. As the goddess of the harvest, Demeter was very important to the ancients. They depended on the land for their food, and any crop failure meant great hardship.
5. Because people traveled from all over Greece, and later the Roman world, the roads had to be safe for travel. Since wars were a common occurrence and battles were fought in the spring, summer, and fall, attendance would have been affected if war was being waged in any of the regions where participants in the mysteries were preparing to travel.
6. Helios, the god of the sun, told Demeter how Hades, the god of the underworld, had fallen in love with Demeter's daughter Persephone and had convinced his brother Zeus to help him kidnap her.
7. Demeter planned to make Demophon immortal. Every night, she fed him ambrosia, the food of the gods, and held his body in the sacred fire, gradually burning out every trace of his human nature. Demeter was heartbroken because she had lost her daughter Persephone. Demophon alleviated her sadness. Perhaps she wanted him to take her daughter's place.
8. While Persephone was with Hades in the underworld, winter reigned (no crops grew, and the land was barren). When Persephone visited Demeter, spring arrived (the trees and crops began to grow). During summer, Demeter and Persephone happily roamed the world together. In autumn, the crops were harvested and farmers prepared for Persephone's departure.
9. In the myth of Demeter and Persephone, the gods have many human characteristics. They are angry, sad, and happy. They pout and are vengeful. Zeus appears as the master, the one in control. Yet he is not above the laws and must abide by them. Persephone cannot leave Hades forever because she ate of the pomegranate in the underworld.

Vesta and the Vestal Virgins

1. Vesta's temple was round, not rectangular.

Some believe this was because Vesta's temple was an imitation of the early Roman round straw huts built around a central hearth. Plutarch, an ancient Greek biographer, wrote that Vesta's temple was round because it represented the entire universe and had a fire, the focus of life, in the middle.

2. Life as a Vestal Virgin gave the priestesses many privileges and honors. They were respected everywhere. Also, since Vestal Virgins had to remain priestesses for a minimum of thirty years, they were approximately forty years old when their mandatory service ended. This was far beyond the marrying age.

The Panathenaic Festival

1. Hephaestos, the god of fire, wished to marry Athena, the goddess of wisdom. Athena had vowed not to marry. Hephaestos then produced a child, Erichthonios, on his own. Athena felt somewhat responsible for this child and saw to his upbringing. In time, she made him king of Athens. Erichthonios believed he owed his good fortune and well-being to Athena. Therefore, he instituted the Panathenaic Festival in her honor.
2. This privilege served several purposes. It made the Athenians feel a tremendous sense of pride for their city-state. It helped give Athenians a common bond. It set Athenians apart from others during the Panathenaic Festival, instituted by a demigod (Erichthonios) in honor of Athena, one of the greatest Olympians.

Saturnus and Saturnalia

1. The Romans credited the god Saturnus with teaching them agriculture. In December, farmers had finished harvesting their crops, so they had time to participate in festivities. Also, on December 25, the Romans had long celebrated the festival of Sol Invictus. This festival reminded them that the darkness of winter would not last forever, that spring would soon arrive and crops again would grow and be harvested, and that Saturnus was watching over the farmers and their fields.
2. During the Golden Age, crops grew and were harvested of their own accord, no one ruled anyone, everyone was content, and fairness reigned. The festivities of Saturnalia tried to duplicate this period: Slaves were set free, masters served their slaves, no wars were started, businesses and schools were closed, and criminals were not executed. It was a time of merriment, equality, and honesty.

QUESTIONS FOR DISCUSSION

1. a) March was the beginning of the combat season. In ancient times, wars were not fought in winter. For the Romans, March heralded the beginning of military campaigns. The Salii were the priests of Mars, the god of war. Therefore, March, the month named for Mars, was the appropriate time for this festival.

   b) April was the month of flower blossoms, sowing crops, and budding trees. Demeter was the goddess of the harvest. Therefore, April was the appropriate time for festivities associated with her worship.

   c) December was a period of short days and long nights. There was little plant growth. Saturnus was the patron of agriculture. Saturnalia was best celebrated in December, when, at the end of the month, the days began to grow longer, promising the coming of spring and the planting of crops.

   d) In the old Roman calendar, March was the first month of the year, February the last. Lupercalia was celebrated to ensure fertility in the new year. Hence, Lupercalia was appropriately celebrated in the last month of the year, as everyone looked to the new year with great optimism.
2. Festivals celebrate beliefs, ideas, and customs. As such, they tend to promote a closer relationship among people who celebrate them. In ancient times, travel was far more time consuming and difficult than it is today. Also, many ancient peoples were farmers, and their work kept them close to home. Festivals allowed a break in their routine and a reason to meet and share with others. Festivals, especially festivals limited to a particular tribe, city-state, or nation, helped to unify those involved. This unity was important to avoid being conquered by larger nations. If a nation was conquered, the regional festivals kept alive a sense of national pride. Festivals whose rituals extended over a period of days especially strengthened the bonds between city-states and peoples and encouraged an exchange of ideas and beliefs.